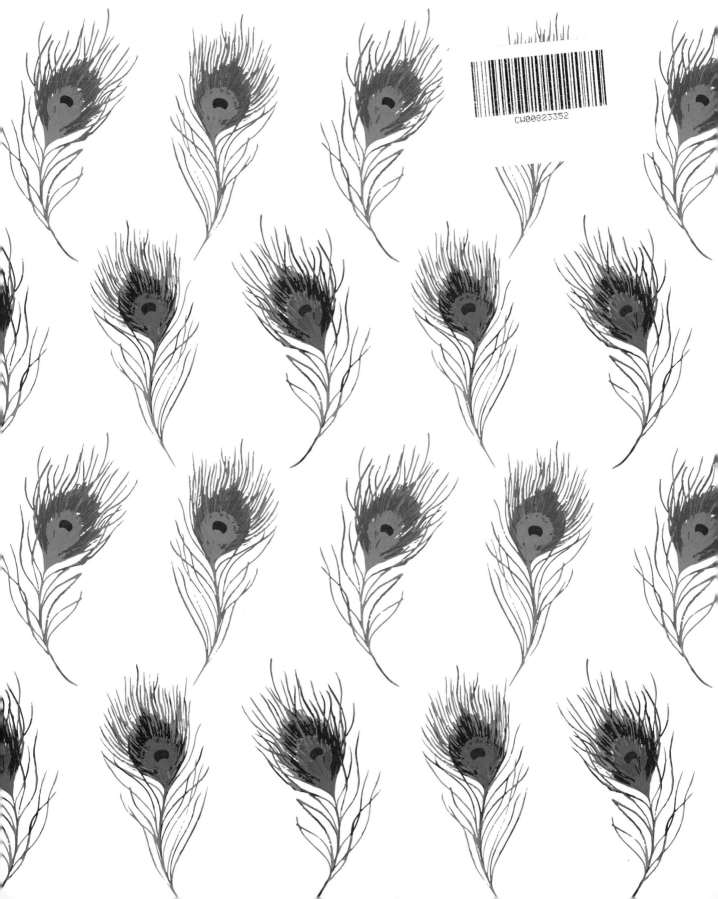

Drag Queen Brunch

A gift to y'all from Naoleans
Cooking School. 3/5/2024.
Strange but hope you enjoy!
xxx
Mummy

Drag Queen Brunch

By Poppy Tooker

with Sam Hanna

New Orleans 2020

Photography by Sam Hanna unless otherwise noted.
Front cover photograph by José A. Guzman Colón
Front cover design by Charlotte Tobin
Back cover photograph by Sally Asher

ISBN: 978-1-941879-27-6

The name and logo for "Rainbow Road Press" are trademarks of Rainbow Road
    Press LLC and are registered with the U.S. Patent and Trademark Office.

For information regarding permission to reproduce selections from this book, write
to Permissions, Rainbow Road Press LLC, PO Box 125, Metairie, Louisiana 70004.

Printed in Korea

Published by Rainbow Road Press
PO Box 125
Metairie, LA 70004
www.rainbowroadpress.com

To the brother of my heart,
Joe Middleton, and
all the Demented Women,
past and present.

The Queens

The Brunch

The Cover Girl and the Cake

My cover girl is Vinsantos Defonte, Drag Mister-ess of the New Orleans Drag Workshop, and that's no cake! It's actually an omelette, more commonly known as a Baked Alaska.

Antoine Alciatore, who founded the nation's oldest continuously operating family-owned restaurant in 1840, was one of the very first to serve this magically cake-encased meringue ice cream bombe in the United States. Antoine mastered the dish, originally called omelette norvégienne, as a young apprentice in France. At Antoine's, he named his creation "Omelette Historiée à la Jules Cesar."

In 1867, New York City's Delmonico's Restaurant (the only restaurant in operation in America today that is older than New Orleans' own Antoine's) created a version that they called Baked Alaska, in honor of the U.S. acquisition of the Alaskan territory. In New Orleans, Antoine's son, Jules, who by then was running his father's restaurant, renamed the dish "Omelette Alaska Antoine."

So as they say in the Treme, "Let's all go get a slice of *that* cake!"

(Courtesy José A. Guzman Colón)

Baked Alaska

Antoine's Restaurant
Serves 6

While Antoine Alciatore was perhaps the first to serve this 19th-century dessert in the Americas, its popularity reached its zenith in the 1950s. Today, Baked Alaska is almost a museum piece, but it continues to be a favorite at Antoine's Restaurant.

1 16-ounce pound cake
1 quart vanilla ice cream
7 large egg whites
½ teaspoon salt
1 cup fine granulated sugar

Slice pound cake into ¾-inch slices. Line the bottom of a 12- to 14-inch oval domed pan with cake slices. Scoop the ice cream onto the cake slices in an oval shape and cover with the remainder of the pound cake slices.

Whip egg whites with salt until they are foamy and hold their shape. Continue whipping, adding sugar gradually, until egg whites are shiny and form stiff peaks. Spread the whipped egg whites to cover the Alaska completely. Smooth with a spatula.

Quickly brown the Alaska with a small kitchen torch or under a broiler flame. Decorate with additional egg whites as desired. To serve, scoop out each portion using 2 large spoons.

Having our cake and eating it too!

(Courtesy José A. Guzman Colón)

Foreword

After celebrating my 20th year working in the art of drag, I suddenly realized it had always been part of my life, I just didn't know that it had a name. My stage career essentially began in third grade, when I donned my first wig to play the lead role of Samson in the epic biblical saga of *Samson and Delilah*. By high school, I was in full-face makeup every day while experimenting with a mixture of both men's and women's clothes.

I became a professional artist in 1998 at a small but wildly successful San Francisco club, Trannyshack, which operated after midnight at the Stud. The Trannyshack proved to be a breeding ground for performers who regarded drag as a personal art form and a means for political action and social justice. It was also a place where drag wasn't defined by the conventional constructs typically associated with the mainstream view of drag performers as female impersonators or the self-deprecating comediennes usually depicted in television and film.

This club was considered "church" to many of us. It was a blender of genders, races, and economic backgrounds, open to any and all political and religious beliefs, resulting in a more cutting edge, radical, and progressive view of drag as performance art.

When I moved to New Orleans in 2010, I hit the ground running as a performer but quickly learned that there wasn't a place in the New Orleans drag scene that featured or accepted my sort of out-of-the-box interpretation of drag. I was quickly adopted into the local scene of burlesque, variety, and musical performers, but I still missed the type of drag family I had known in San Francisco.

That is how in 2013, I became Head Mister-ess, founding the New Orleans Drag Workshop. Friends helped get the word out through an online submission call to the community, and news of the workshop spread. What happened next was truly an incredible surprise. People signed up! People I had never met. People with dreams of doing drag on all levels, from the most traditional to the most avant-garde.

The workshop is a 10-week intensive tutorial covering everything from the fundamentals of putting a look and a character together through the ideals that I uphold as a seasoned performer. While instructing students in clever crafts like how to create curves from sofa cushions, I also share what it takes to create and execute powerful and memorable performance art, along with imparting the nuts and bolts of the drag side of the entertainment biz. This all culminates with the students' "draguation," live on stage in front of a few hundred people.

Our yearly competition, The Miss Pageant Pageant, pits the strongest performers who have completed the workshop against each other, pushing them to create the best versions of themselves.

It has become clear that we are on to something that's so much more than just a fun way for people to express themselves. The workshop has become a truly transformative experience that changes the lives and minds of not only the workshop members, but their audiences as well.

Today, my drag-uates number more than 100, but when I began this adventure, I imagined it would only be for the fringe and outcast performers with whom I self-identified. Amazingly, through this cross-cultural experiment, a completely new character has emerged, that of the reluctant drag mother. She expands my understanding and acceptance of the vast nuances that make up the New Orleans drag scene. Bridges from Bywater to the French Quarter have been built. Walls have been torn down. Families have been created while careers and opportunities once unobtainable have been achieved. The New Orleans Drag Workshop has played a role in the Crescent City's emergence as one of the most important drag communities in the world today.

I'm honored to be at the forefront of this cultural movement and even more honored to be cover girl of a book that intellectually, visually, and culturally ties the world of drag to an historic New Orleans tradition.

My greatest truth? Everyone has their own inner diva and simply must do whatever it takes to release her magic into the universe. Oh, and a girl's gotta eat!

Vinsantos Defonte

For J. M. Begne
a reminder of
Julian Eltin
2-10-1

Introduction

Almost forgotten in time, Julian Eltinge once was arguably the greatest star of early 20th-century America. From the early 1900s through the 1930s, he rarely appeared on stage dressed as a man. Julian maneuvered the world of drag with humor, often playing characters forced to dress as females in order to accomplish some goal. Many were not even aware Julian was a man. In the film *The Isle of Love*, his beauty was even deemed a match for silent movie star Rudolph Valentino. Eventually, Julian became one of the highest paid actors of his time.

Off stage, he worked hard to display a masculine persona, participating in staged boxing matches and smoking cigars. The ladies adored him. He published a women's magazine filled with "beauty hints and tips," where he promoted his own line of cosmetics. One ad featuring Julian as a beautiful woman read, "See what the Julian Eltinge Cold Cream does for a man? Imagine what it will do for a woman!" Satirist Dorothy Parker referred to Julian and his alter ego, Vesta Tilly, as "ambi-sexterous." But when challenged about his sexuality, he was known to proclaim, "I'm not gay, I just like pearls."

When Julian traveled to New Orleans with his stage show, he never missed an opportunity to dine at Begue's. The elaborate five-course meal served daily there, at exactly 11 a.m., was originally intended for the French Market butchers, whose stalls were located just across Decatur Street from the restaurant. But by the late 19th century, tourists had discovered Madame Begue's delectable brunch, and reservations were always at a premium.

After dining there on February 10, 1917, Julian Eltinge left behind two autographed photos. In one, he appears resplendent in tiara and pearls. The photo is signed, "For M. Begue—Just a line to say better than ever and after fourteen years." In the second, a winsome Julian peeks out from under a broad-brimmed straw hat. He inscribed it, "A reminder of Julian Eltinge."

After Madame Begue's death, the famous location became Tujague's Restaurant, and somehow Julian Eltinge's sepia-tinted photo continued to hang in the dining room of the famous Decatur Street location for almost a century. In the summer of 2013, Tujague's owner, Mark Latter, had the Begue Room painted. Julian's photo was removed in the process and stored away in the building's third floor attic. Soon, it became clear that the spirit of Julian Eltinge was not taking the banishment well.

Later that same year, Ian Wrin and his fiancée, April Russ, were vacationing in New Orleans when they enjoyed a meal in the Begue Room at Tujague's. They snapped a selfie to remember the moment, but upon returning home, they were startled to discover a ghostly image in the photo, peering out from the same corner where Julian Eltinge's photo had hung for more than a century. Once Julian's photo was returned to its former place of prominence in the dining room, the ghostly sightings ceased.

When *Tujague's Cookbook* was published in 2015, complete with the captured image of Julian's ghost, his story gained new traction. In Julian's honor, Tujague's began hosting what came to be known as Poppy's Pop Up Drag Queen Brunches, benefiting CrescentCare, the 21st-century iteration of the nonprofit formerly known as the NO/AIDS Task Force. The generous drag queens even donated their tips, which often exceeded $1,000 at a time!

Whether their style leans towards classic beauty pageant glamour or the more politically and socially tinged performances favored by some newer girls on the circuit, New Orleans drag queens entertain their hearts out for wildly diverse brunch audiences for birthdays, bachelors and bachelorettes, and even families with children.

This book is intended to curate the beauty and tell the delicious tales of drag queens past and present. Let's dance together through these rollicking pages and savor every last bite!

JULIAN ELTINGE
(Courtesy Tujague's Restaurant)

The ghost of Julian Eltinge photobombs Ian Wrin and his fiancée April Russ at Tujague's. (Courtesy Tujague's Restaurant)

Madame Begue's Stuffed Eggs

Begue's Exchange

Serves 6

This version of stuffed eggs originated with Madame Begue, who used butter instead of mayonnaise. When Julian Eltinge dined on this elegant version at her restaurant, he surely used a fork and knife.

6 hardboiled eggs, peeled
2 tablespoons butter, softened
1 carrot, boiled till tender
Salt and pepper to taste
1½ cups loosely packed watercress
6 slices cold ham

Cut eggs in half. Remove yolk and set aside egg white. In a small bowl, mash together egg yolk and softened butter. Cut carrot into a fine dice. Stir into yolk mixture, season with salt and pepper, and stuff into egg white. Serve eggs at room temperature on a bed of watercress with cold, sliced ham.

How It Was:
Drag in New Orleans

RuPaul famously said, "We're all born naked and the rest is drag." Does that make us all drag queens? Hardly. But her point is well made. Once we are old enough to choose how we want to express ourselves publicly through our clothing and attitude, there are an infinite number of ways to go.

The drag "queen" has been around in one form or another for centuries. Shakespeare and his contemporaries used male actors in female roles. Eighteenth-century England saw the rise of the "macaroni," a foppish man who wore exaggeratedly stylish and often androgynous clothing and behaved and spoke in an affected manner. And what of the drag "king"? Female physicians in the 19th century occasionally wore masculine clothing. Inspired by the fight for women's suffrage, Amelia Bloomer made the "bloomer" fashion famous by wearing exposed pantalettes over a loose blouse or tunic.

And what of New Orleans Carnival and its connection to drag? It is important to differentiate among drag, female impersonation, and cross-dressing. In the late 1800s and early 1900s, cross-dressing was a popular Carnival costume for both men and women. After all, Mardi Gras was the day when all inhibitions and rules were lifted and all means of self-expression, even those that were provocative and possibly illegal, were on display. The term "promiscuous maskers" was assigned to those who appeared on the street in costume rather than on floats with a krewe. The term carried a slightly pejorative meaning, suggesting that street masking was relegated to the middle and lower classes who were unafraid of attracting attention to themselves. Men and women commonly dressed as the opposite sex on Mardi Gras, not to get their jollies and not to perform but to take advantage of the opportunity that the day afforded for being something other than what they were the other 364 days of the year. Even with this sense of public bravery, cross-dressers almost always wore masks to hide their identity.

As the 20th century evolved, New Orleans witnessed the rise of the female impersonator. This term applied to men who performed as women but did not dress in drag outside the confines of a music club. The earliest known club for female impersonators in the city was called the Wonder Club. Opened in the early 1930s in the first block of Decatur Street, the Wonder Club employed female impersonators who dressed elegantly and sang popular songs in their own voices. The hard-working performers put on shows at 10 p.m., midnight, and 2 a.m. Feeling the sting of police harassment, proprietor Emile Morlet moved the club to the West End, far away from downtown, in a building set on pilings over the water of Lake Pontchartrain and renamed the club the Wonder Bar.

In the late 1940s, the Wonder Bar was taken over by perhaps the most famous female impersonators club in the city's history, the Club My-O-My. Continuing the tradition of showcasing elegant men performing in glamorous women's clothing, Club My-O-My became so popular that tour companies took hordes of tourists by bus to the edge of Lake Pontchartrain to witness the performances by such luminaries as Gene La Marr, Poppy Lane, and Jimmy Callaway. With the slogan "The World's Most Beautiful Boys in Women's Attire," Club My-O-My remained popular until a fire in 1972 destroyed the building. The club moved into the French Quarter for a few years but never regained its former popularity.

And what of real drag queens? What counted as a drag queen in New Orleans and how was that identity connected to Carnival? Beginning in the 1930s, public transvestism was illegal except on Fat Tuesday. Naturally this meant that anyone choosing to dress as the opposite sex for any reason was limited to Mardi Gras. Gay men who enjoyed dressing as women and adopting female behavior (and to a lesser degree, women who dressed as men) were limited to house parties for their mutual entertainment, that is, until the birth of the first gay krewe.

Drag queen house parties and balls in private homes were enjoyed in secret by gay men and lesbians in the mid-20th century. One of these house parties was thrown by Douglas Jones in his home on South Carrollton Avenue. He invited his friends to his home, all or most dressed in drag, and any who wished could watch the Krewe of Carrollton parade pass by his house. In the spirit of creating a Carnival organization like Carrollton and so many others, he declared his 1958 party to be hosted by the Krewe of Yuga, thereby inaugurating the first gay krewe in New Orleans.

His 1959 ball was such a success that in 1960 he moved the event to a club on the lakefront to accommodate the growing crowds. In 1961, the ball took place at the Rambler Room in Metairie, a dance studio attached to an elementary school. Every year the Krewe of Yuga chose a queen, proclaimed Yuga Regina, and assigned a few members to the court as maids. At the 1962 ball, when the ball was in full swirl and anticipating the crowning of famous French Quarter antiquarian Elmo Avet as Yuga Regina V, officers from the Jefferson Parish Sheriff's Office raided the ball and arrested nearly 100 men, declaring the event to be a "lewd stag party." Following police culture of the era, the men who were arrested saw their names and home addresses published in the newspapers, causing no end of personal losses as well as the end of the Krewe of Yuga.

Happily, the same year that the Krewe of Yuga ball came to an abrupt end, a new krewe was born, giving drag queens another safe place to congregate and celebrate. The Krewe of Petronius hosted their first ball in 1962 and continue the pageantry to this day. Pioneers like Bill Woolley, Carlos Rodriguez, JoJo Landry, Bill McKenzie, and others formed this krewe after seeing the early success of Yuga. These men wanted to take the appreciation for drag and costumes to an even higher level. In a move to both legitimize themselves and protect themselves from police harassment, the Krewe of Petronius became the first gay krewe to obtain a state charter.

In the wake of the formation of Petronius, new krewes with a bent toward drag popped up, including Amon-Ra, Ganymede, Armeinius, Apollo, Olympus, and many others. With the law against public cross-dressing abolished in the 1970s, there was no end to the opportunities for drag queens to thrive in the city. In the mid-1980s, more than a dozen gay krewes happily co-existed. Perhaps it is underappreciated how strong and supportive the relationships were among some krewes, which helped lead to this explosion in numbers.

The AIDS crisis affected the community deeply. Krewes lost one member after another, and others naturally turned their attention and their pocketbooks to caring for ailing loved ones. Nonetheless, four krewes managed to hold on during this time: Petronius, Amon-Ra, Armeinius, and Lords of Leather. These four krewes understandably dedicated more time than ever before to fundraising for charities like Lazarus House, and drag queens were a huge part of this philanthropic effort. Money raised during their performances in bars often went to these crucial causes, and this spirit of charity continues among today's drag community.

So where is drag now? There is great joy in seeing new generations of drag queens emerge. Drag performance artist Vinsantos Defonte has developed a drag workshop to train young draglings. The Sisters of Perpetual Indulgence continue to grow in numbers and influence. More and more clubs and venues are fostering connections to drag and are showcasing sold-out performances. And no doubt *RuPaul's Drag Race* has enlightened a whole new audience as to the extraordinary creativity and wit of the drag queen. But there is no doubt that as long as we have Mardi Gras, we will be blessed with the charm and magnetism of the drag queen.

Wayne Phillips
Curator of Costumes and Textiles
Curator of Carnival Collections
Louisiana State Museum

A Word from CrescentCare

What could be more fun than a drag show? Drag and brunch together! We owe a debt of gratitude to many of our community's entertainers, those often unsung performers who are heroes/heroines in our eyes. When the AIDS epidemic began in the early 1980s, it was the drag queens of New Orleans who threw some of the first fundraisers to benefit the NO/AIDS Task Force.

In those early days, we had few services to offer and even fewer answers to give. Over the years the NO/AIDS Task Force has grown to include more than 30 programs and services for the community. In 2014, the NO/AIDS Task Force broadened its mission and took on the CrescentCare brand in order to expand our healthcare outreach to the entire LGBTQ community. Our commitment to serving those with HIV, while seeking an end to the disease, remains unwavering.

Today, drag performers still play an important role in raising dollars for HIV services and awareness. Joining forces with these entertainers, Poppy Tooker has been a champion and tireless supporter of our agency as a spokesperson for Dining Out for Life®, the most important annual fundraiser for our Food for Friends program. Poppy believes in the important work we do to feed those with HIV (and now cancer) in the Greater New Orleans community. We are grateful for her leadership and for being the hostess of the best drag brunches in New Orleans.

Here's to you, Poppy, and the great drag ladies who make our brunches special! Thanks for making CrescentCare the benefactor of your important work.

Noel Twilbeck
Chief Executive Officer, CrescentCare

Tujague's Drag Queen Brunch

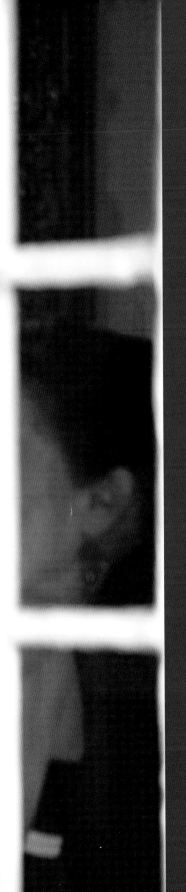

Debbie with a D

Something magical happens when you're in drag in New Orleans.

Whether she's a platinum blonde channeling Marilyn Monroe or rocking a cotton candy pink wig, Debbie with a D's drag comes from a deep place of consideration.

Growing up in a Pentecostal church in Baltimore, Debbie was taught that any form of cross-dressing was a sin. Drag shows became the sanctuary she lost when the church rejected her for being gay. Now drag is her own personal statement: a rebellion against oppression, stigma, and the patriarchy and religion that claims if you aren't a certain kind of "normal," you're unfit to be loved.

To know Debbie is to love her. As a child, her favorite book was *Anne of Green Gables*, so in an homage to Anne with an E, she became Debbie with a D.

Debbie sees drag as a crucial art form that creates a space for social, political, and personal expression, a space that can turn personal and social turmoil into power and strength. As she uses storytelling to explore emotion, the stage becomes an artistic outlet. Past pain is exposed while allowing the young Debbie and those like her a safe space to heal and grow.

"Something magical happens when you're in drag in New Orleans' French Quarter. It's better than live theatre," Debbie says with a gentle smile and a nod of her head.

Three Little Pigs

Tujague's Restaurant

Chef Thomas Robby

Serves 4

All the little piggies show up for this delicious dish, created especially for Tujague's Drag Queen Brunch.

Hash

2 tablespoons olive oil

8 ounces thick-cut bacon,
   cut into ½-inch dice

8 ounces andouille, sliced
   into half-moons, ¼ inch thick

8 ounces smoked sausage,
   sliced into half-moons, ¼ inch thick

3 large Yukon Gold potatoes,
   diced and blanched

¼ cup sliced green onions

1 teaspoon minced garlic

Salt and black pepper to taste

Spicy Hollandaise

4 egg yolks

½ cup butter, melted

1 tablespoon lemon juice

Pinch of salt

Pinch of cayenne

1 tablespoon hot sauce

Remaining Ingredients

8 poached eggs (or fried or
   scrambled) (see page 61)

Heat oil in a heavy saucepan over medium heat. Add bacon and fry until crispy on the edges. Add the sausages and cook for 5 minutes. Mix in the potatoes, green onions, and garlic. Cook over a medium heat until potatoes start to break down and the mixture begins to stick together. Season with salt and pepper.

Meanwhile, in a stainless-steel bowl, whisk the egg yolks and lemon juice together. Place bowl over a pot of simmering water and continue whisking rapidly until mixture doubles in size and begins to thicken. Slowly drizzle in butter, whisking continuously until fully incorporated. Season with salt, cayenne, and hot sauce. Keep warm.

To serve, divide hash into 4 bowls. Top each bowl with 2 poached eggs and Spicy Hollandaise. Serve immediately.

Poppy's Pink Drink

Serves 1

My pink drink saves the day when trying to keep up with a bevy of drag queens! It looks so festive and refreshing that everyone wants to know what Poppy's drinking.

8 ounces chilled sparkling water

10 dashes (approximately ½ ounce) Peychaud's bitters

Wedge of lime

Pour chilled sparkling water into a stemmed glass. Shake in 10 generous dashes of Peychaud's bitters and garnish with a squeeze of fresh lime.

Bananas Foster

Brennan's

Serves 4

Bananas Foster was created in 1951 when Brennan's founder, Owen Brennan, urged his sister Ella to create a flaming dessert using the bananas that were flooding through the Port of New Orleans. The resulting dish has become the world's most famous flaming dessert. But on first tasting it, Owen reportedly asked Ella why she'd "ruined the dish with vanilla ice cream." Maybe he'd enjoy it Drag Queen Brunch style: on Pain Perdu!

¼ cup unsalted butter

1 cup brown sugar

½ teaspoon ground cinnamon

¼ cup banana liqueur

4 bananas, cut in half lengthwise, then halved

¼ cup dark rum

4 scoops vanilla ice cream

Combine butter, sugar, and cinnamon in a large sauté pan. Place pan over low heat and cook, stirring, until sugar dissolves. Stir in banana liqueur, then add bananas to the pan. When bananas soften and begin to brown, carefully add rum. Continue to cook sauce until rum is hot, then tip pan slightly to ignite the alcohol. When flames subside, lift bananas out of pan and place 4 pieces over each serving of ice cream. Generously spoon warm sauce over ice cream and serve immediately.

We made this!

Pain Perdu

Serves 4

New Orleans French bread becomes stale within a day, so thrifty Creoles saved the otherwise "lost bread" by serving Pain Perdu for breakfast the next day. Pain Perdu can be topped with fresh berries and powdered sugar, drenched in cane syrup, or Drag Queen Brunch style, topped with flaming Bananas Foster.

4 eggs
1½ cups milk
4 tablespoons sugar
2 teaspoons vanilla
12 slices stale French bread,
    cut 1½ inches thick
6 tablespoons butter

In a shallow bowl, mix together eggs, milk, sugar, and vanilla. Soak each slice of bread in milk mixture so that the bread is moist but does not fall apart. Drain bread and set aside.

Melt butter in a frying pan over medium-high heat. Fry moistened bread in butter until browned on both sides. Serve with favorite topping.

Bananas Foster Martini

Ralph's on the Park

Serves 1

This whimsical cocktail has all the flavor and heritage of the Brennan family's most famous flaming dessert. Best of all, you can have your Bananas Foster and drink one too!

1½ ounces Absolut Vanilla vodka

1 dash spiced rum

1 ounce crème de banana

½ ounce butterscotch schnapps

1 splash cream

Nutmeg to taste

1 banana slice for garnish

Combine all ingredients in a cocktail shaker with ice. Serve up in a martini glass. Sprinkle with nutmeg and garnish with a banana slice.

Mistie Bonet

All sorts are welcome.

With a drag name drawn from the enchanted world of Pokémon, Mistie Bonet is an anime character sprung to life, complete with the legs of a showgirl. From the top of her pink fairy floss tresses to the tips of her gold-sequined platform boots, Mistie's "wow" factor is always in overdrive. Even when an auburn-tressed Mistie appears regally draped in purple velvet, her cat eyes flash.

Outrageous hair color was her entree into drag, but a passion for cosmetics soon overtook the hair mania. As her makeup glides on, Mistie feels her confidence grow along with her lengthening eyelashes.

Tapped to organize her own shows, Mistie is busy creating an alternative drag scene of her own with a cadre of up-and-coming young performers. Her credo remains total inclusivity: all sorts are welcome.

Crabmeat Cheesecake

Palace Café

Serves 8

When the Palace Café first served this savory cheesecake in 1991, the idea was radical. Today, their Crabmeat Cheesecake, topped with a luscious, buttery meunière sauce, has become a modern Creole classic.

Pecan Crust

¾ cup pecans

1 cup all-purpose flour

¼ teaspoon salt

5 tablespoons chilled butter

3 tablespoons ice water

Filling

½ cup finely diced onion

1 tablespoon butter

4 ounces crabmeat

8 ounces cream cheese,
   room temperature

⅓ cup Creole cream cheese
   or sour cream

2 eggs

1 tablespoon hot sauce

Kosher salt and white pepper to taste

Meunière Sauce

1 lemon, peeled and quartered

½ cup Worcestershire sauce

½ cup hot sauce

¼ cup heavy whipping cream

¼ cup chilled butter, cut into small cubes

Kosher salt and white pepper to taste

Garnish

2 cups sliced mixed wild mushrooms

3 tablespoons butter (room temperature),
   divided

24 crab claw fingers

Pecan Crust

Preheat oven to 350 degrees. Finely grind pecans in a food processor. Add flour and salt. Mix well. Transfer to a large mixing bowl and cut in butter, working butter into flour with 2 knives until dough is in crumbs the size of small peas. Add ice water and evenly incorporate into the mixture. The mixture will remain fairly crumbly. Roll out dough to a ⅛-inch thickness on a lightly floured surface. Press dough into a greased 9-inch tart pan, starting with the sides and working toward the bottom. Bake crust for 20 minutes, until golden brown.

Filling

In a medium pan, sauté onion in butter until translucent. Add crabmeat and cook until just heated through. Remove from heat and set aside.

In a mixer fitted with a paddle, or by hand using a wooden spoon, blend cream cheese until smooth. Add Creole cream cheese and mix well. Mix in eggs one at a time. Gently fold in crabmeat mixture. Stir in hot sauce and season to taste with salt and white pepper. Spoon into prepared crust. Bake at 300 degrees for 30-40 minutes, or until firm to the touch.

Meunière Sauce

Combine lemon, Worcestershire sauce, and hot sauce in heavy saucepot. Reduce over medium heat, stirring constantly with a wire whisk until mixture becomes thick and syrupy. Whisk in heavy whipping cream. Reduce heat to low and slowly blend in butter, one cube at a time, adding additional butter only after each cube has completely incorporated into the sauce. Remove from heat and continue to stir. Season with salt and pepper to taste.

Sauté mushrooms in 2 tablespoons butter until tender and all moisture has cooked off. Excess water from the mushrooms may break your sauce if it isn't cooked off. Stir mushrooms into meunière sauce.

Melt 1 tablespoon butter in sauté pan and warm crab claws over low heat. Slice cheesecake and top each piece with warm meunière sauce and 3 crab claws.

Ramos Gin Fizz

Serves 1

Henry Ramos, the creator of this creamy breakfast cocktail, employed dozens of shaker boys at his early-20th-century New Orleans bar to handle the demand for the gin fizz.

1 teaspoon powdered sugar
3 dashes orange flower water
½ ounce fresh squeezed lemon juice
¼ ounce fresh squeezed lime juice
1 egg white
1 ounce gin
2½ ounces milk

Fill a cocktail shaker ⅓ full of ice cubes. Add ingredients to the shaker in the order listed. Cover and shake thoroughly to mix all ingredients into a creamy and foamy smoothness. Strain into a tall glass and serve.

Jessica Champagne

Once you pop the cork, it's all over!

This statuesque beauty describes herself as "just like a bottle of bubbly—because once you pop the cork, it's all over!" The self-dubbed Queen of Slay loves to slay audiences and has been successfully doing so for more than 20 years.

Elegance personified, Miss Jessica Champagne prides herself on being a role model for today's new drag queens, opening doors for young girls who need encouragement. She advises, "Invest in your drag so people can see you're proud of what you do." Her reward comes from seeing the spirit of drag pass on from one queen to another.

Mimosa

Serves 1

As if you need instructions for a mimosa! You'll be making these by the pitcher-full before the party gets started!

6 ounces champagne
2 ounces orange juice
¼ ounce Cointreau

Pour champagne into a flute. Add orange juice and top with Cointreau.

Poinsettia

Serves 1

When pink rules the day!

6 ounces champagne
2 ounces cranberry juice

Pour champagne into a flute. Top with cranberry juice.

French 75

Serves 1

When a mimosa just isn't enough.

1½ tablespoons lemon juice
2 ounces gin
1 tablespoon simple syrup
4 ounces champagne

Combine lemon juice, gin, and simple syrup over ice in a shaker. Shake vigorously and strain into a flute. Top with champagne.

Lobster & Tasso Eggs Benedict

Ralph's on the Park

Chef Chip Flanagan

Serves 4

Legend has it that Louisiana crawfish began as lobsters that shrunk in size during the long trip south from Nova Scotia with the Acadians. Real Cajun tasso marries Atlantic lobster over a flaky, hot biscuit for this over-the-top Drag Queen Brunch dish.

¼ cup thinly sliced tasso, julienne cut, + ½ cup thinly sliced tasso

1 tablespoon olive oil

4 teaspoons butter

4 biscuits, halved

½ pound cooked lobster meat

8 poached eggs (see page 61)

1½ cups Jalapeño Hollandaise (recipe follows)

Preheat oven to 400 degrees. Toss ¼ cup julienned tasso in olive oil, then spread on a baking sheet. Bake for 5 minutes until just crisp. Set aside.

Melt butter in a skillet and quickly sauté the ½ cup sliced tasso until heated. Top each biscuit half with tasso. In the same skillet, gently heat the lobster meat. Place warm, poached eggs on top of the biscuits and tasso. Spoon hollandaise over the eggs and top with lobster. Garnish with a crown of crisp, julienned tasso.

Jalapeño Hollandaise

Yields 1½ cups

1 teaspoon lemon juice

4 egg yolks

½ pound butter, melted

2 tablespoons roasted, peeled, seeded, and diced jalapeño pepper

1 pinch salt

1 pinch cayenne pepper

Combine lemon juice and egg yolks in a stainless-steel bowl. Place bowl over a pot of simmering water and whisk until thick and fluffy. Slowly drizzle in butter, continuously whisking until fully incorporated. Remove from heat and stir in diced jalapeño. Season with salt and cayenne. Keep sauce warm until ready to serve.

Princess Mina's Quiche

Flamingos Café

Serves 6

Flamingos Café was an immediate sensation when Paul Doll and Tom Struve put the wildly gay culture of the late 1970s on display in New Orleans' Garden District. Camp was *de rigueur* there. Even the cook was a drag queen!

Brunch reigned day and night, with fluffy omelettes, dainty quiche, and crispy salads served in huge, glistening clamshells as the bill of fare. The cocktail menu included "A Hole in One," which commenced with a high proof shot and ended with a piercing—usually of an ear lobe—right there at the bar!

Draped in a shimmering sari with a huge, gleaming ruby adorning her forehead, the beautiful East Indian Princess Mina worked by day as a "Chef-ette" at Flamingos Café. The exotic beauty folded fluffy omelettes and crafted clever quiches there. "Oh, my man I love him sooooooo . . ." she would trill while throwing scraps to the courtyard cats.

8 crisp slices thick-cut bacon, crumbled

⅓ cup finely chopped onion

1 cup grated Swiss cheese

1 9-inch pie crust

2 cups half-and-half

4 eggs

¼ teaspoon salt

⅛ teaspoon black pepper

Hot sauce to taste

Preheat oven to 350 degrees. Mix together the bacon, onion, and Swiss cheese and spread into prepared pie crust. In a separate bowl, mix together half-and-half, eggs, salt, pepper, and hot sauce. Pour into pie crust. Bake for 40-45 minutes, or until a toothpick inserted in the center comes out clean. Allow to cool for 15-20 minutes before serving.

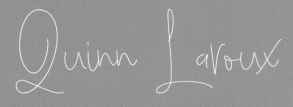

Quinn Laroux

I'm every woman.

Slim and sexy with an Audrey Hepburn style, Quinn Laroux takes her drag very seriously. Two years after her "draguation," Quinn's drag has developed into a personal art form highly political in nature.

With a taste for biting satire, Quinn's take on "Twenty-Three and Me" begins bilingually in French and German before morphing into additional tongues. That wild set concludes with the definitive "I'm Every Woman," answering that question once and for all.

Quinn's ambitious one-woman performance, "It's Fine," uses comedy to heal old hurts, an experience she describes as a "heavy mood swing," while "Sexy Cat" allows Quinn to become just that—a very sexy cat!

This Tennessee native embraced her new hometown with such studied enthusiasm that she founded NOLA Drag Tours, giving tourists and locals alike a taste of drag life in New Orleans' French Quarter. "It's so exciting to take my academic passion for queer history and transform it into entertainment for paying audiences on the streets of New Orleans!"

Sidecar Number 1

Commander's Palace

Serves 1

Although said to be French in origin, the Sidecar is believed to have been inspired by the Brandy Crusta, invented in mid-18th-century New Orleans. Commander's Palace self-proclaimed "Cocktail Chicks," Ti Martin and Lally Brennan, are on a mission to revive this fabulous old cocktail. Try one and you'll be happy to join their mission!

1 tablespoon superfine sugar

1 lemon wedge

2 ounces domestic brandy

1 ounce Cointreau

½ ounce fresh lemon juice

1 lemon twist

Place sugar in a shallow dish or saucer. Wet half of the inside and outside rims of a stemmed cocktail glass with the lemon wedge, then discard the wedge. Dip the rim into the sugar. Fill the glass with ice and set aside.

In a cocktail shaker with ice, combine the brandy, Cointreau, and lemon juice and shake vigorously. Twist the lemon peel into the prepared glass and strain the cocktail over it. Serve immediately.

Creole Cream Cheese

Yields 8 pints

This soft, single-curd fresh cheese has been a favorite at breakfast and brunch since the earliest days of New Orleans. Since its 21st-century resurgence, Creole cream cheese has been featured in sweet and savory dishes across the Crescent City.

1 gallon skim milk
1 cup buttermilk
Pinch of salt
6-8 drops liquid vegetable rennet

In a large stainless or glass bowl, mix together all ingredients. Cover lightly with plastic wrap and leave out at room temperature for 18-24 hours. A single large cheese curd, floating in whey, will form.

With a slotted spoon, transfer large pieces of the cheese into pint-sized cheese molds (or make your own by poking holes in plastic pint containers with a soldering iron). Place molds over a rack in a roasting pan and cover lightly with plastic wrap. Refrigerate for 6-8 hours, allowing cheese to drain, before turning out of molds and storing in a tightly covered container in the refrigerator for up to 2 weeks.

To serve, pour a bit of cream or half-and-half on top and sprinkle with sugar or eat savory style, sprinkled with kosher salt and freshly ground black pepper.

Laveau Contraire

I found a new art form.

Laveau Contraire danced into the world of drag queens in 2015, entering Tumblr's Drag Race, an internet competition fashioned after *RuPaul's Drag Race*. "It was the best decision ever," she recalls. "I won first place and found a new art form in the process."

When it came to choosing her drag name, Laveau was searching for something that called to mind a strong woman, a magical woman. New Orleans' Voodoo queen Marie Laveau was all of that. "Contraire" indicates the contrary forces at work when a man appears in the world as a beautiful woman.

Once she had a taste for drag, Laveau "super nova-ed" her way onto the stage. She plans her performances to include something magical, like the surprise of a wig pulled mysteriously from a sleeve.

Although she warns, "It's challenging to stay disciplined living the life of a fulltime drag queen," the rewards are limitless. "Drag means constantly growing, constantly re-creating, and re-inventing. I'm inspired to bring more joy into lives and not take it all too seriously."
(Courtesy Sally Asher)

Calas

Yields 1 dozen

These fried rice cakes came to New Orleans from Africa via the slave trade. They were sold in the streets by slaves and free people of color and were heralded by the street call of "Calas, calas! Belle calas tout chaud, Madame." In their sweet, original version, they are much like beignets but easier and faster to make!

2 cups cooked rice
6 tablespoons flour
3 heaping tablespoons sugar
2 teaspoons baking powder
¼ teaspoon salt
2 eggs
¼ teaspoon vanilla
Vegetable oil for deep frying
Confectioners' sugar

In a bowl, combine rice, flour, sugar, baking powder, and salt. Mix until rice is thoroughly coated. Add eggs and vanilla and mix well.

In a deep fryer, heat vegetable oil to 360 degrees. Carefully drop rice mixture by spoonfuls into hot oil and fry until brown. Remove from oil with a slotted spoon and drain on paper towels. Sprinkle with confectioners' sugar. Serve hot.

Legs & Eggs

SoBou

Serves 4

There's a lot more than duck legs on display at SoBou's legendary Legs & Eggs brunch!

4 duck legs
Salt and pepper to taste
Sliced orange, grapefruit, or
    other citrus

Preheat oven to 425 degrees. Season duck with salt and pepper. In a cast-iron skillet over medium-low heat, sear duck skin side down for 10 minutes, or until well browned. Flip and brown for 5 minutes. Cover with foil and place skillet in oven. Roast duck for 30 minutes. Uncover and cook an additional 30 minutes, or until a meat thermometer reads 180 degrees when inserted into the thickest part of the leg. Serve each duck leg with a poached egg, nestled into a spoonful of grits, and lightly drizzled with Grand Marnier syrup. Garnish with citrus slices.

Grits

Yields 4 cups

1 tablespoon unsalted butter
¼ cup onion, cut into very small dice
4 cups skim milk
¼ teaspoon kosher salt
⅛ teaspoon white pepper
1 cup stone-ground grits
1 tablespoon chopped thyme leaves
4 green onions, thinly sliced

Heat butter in a 3-quart saucepan over medium heat. Add onion and cook until translucent, about 4 minutes, stirring frequently. Stir in milk and season with salt and pepper. Bring to a simmer, stirring occasionally. Add the grits and mix well to blend. Bring to a boil and cook for about 2 minutes. Reduce heat and simmer 20-30 minutes, stirring frequently, until the grits thicken. Stir in thyme. Cover, remove from heat, and rest for 10 minutes before serving. Season with salt and white pepper to taste.

Poached Eggs

Serves 4

1 teaspoon vinegar
1 teaspoon salt
4 eggs

In a 3-quart saucepan over medium heat, combine 6 cups cold water, vinegar, and salt. Bring to a gentle simmer, then reduce heat to low. Break 1 egg into a small ramekin. Gently pour egg into simmering water. Let egg white set for 1 minute. Using a rubber spatula, carefully lift egg from bottom of the pan and roll slightly in the water. Cook until white is firm and yolk is runny, about 6 minutes. Remove egg with a slotted spoon. Repeat process with remaining eggs.

Grand Marnier Syrup

Yields ½ cup

½ cup sugar
¼ cup water
2 tablespoons Grand Marnier

Combine sugar and water in a saucepan. Bring to a boil and cook for 5 minutes or until syrupy. Remove from heat; let cool to room temperature and stir in Grand Marnier.

Grillades & Grits

Serves 6

With its spicy tomato gravy simmering round steak into tender bites, this classic New Orleans dish graces Creole tables from late night breakfasts to mid-afternoon brunches in the Crescent City.

2 pounds round steak (beef or veal)
½ cup flour + flour for dredging
½ cup oil, divided
1 onion, chopped
3 stalks celery, chopped
1 bell pepper, chopped
15 ounces canned tomato purée
1 bottle of beer
3 cloves garlic
½ teaspoon thyme
1 bay leaf
1 bunch green onions, thinly sliced
Salt, pepper, and hot sauce to taste

Portion round steaks into individual servings and pound thin between sheets of waxed paper. Lightly dredge in flour. Heat 2 tablespoons oil in sauté pan. Brown round steaks on both sides, then remove from pan, and reserve. Add remainder of oil to pan and stir in ½ cup flour to make a roux. Cook until roux reaches the color of milk chocolate. Add onion and cook for 2 minutes, until roux darkens to a bittersweet chocolate color. Mix in celery and bell pepper and cook for another 2 minutes. Stir in tomato purée, beer, garlic, thyme, and bay leaf. Bring to a simmer then return the round steaks to the pan. Cover and simmer for 25-30 minutes, until fork tender. Add green onions and season with salt, pepper, and hot sauce to taste. Serve over grits (see page 61).

Caribbean Milk Punch

Brennan's

Serves 1

New Orleans' favorite breakfast drink, milk punch, usually gets its wallop from bourbon or brandy. At Brennan's, in a nod to our Caribbean neighbors, dark rum from the islands dominates the drink.

1 ounce dark rum
½ ounce bourbon whiskey
1 ounce vanilla bean infused simple syrup
1 ounce heavy cream
Grated nutmeg for garnish

Combine all ingredients in a mixing glass with ice. Shake until frothy and strain into a coupe with no ice. Garnish with nutmeg.

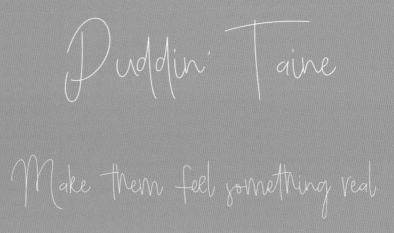

Puddin' Taine

Make them feel something real

Born and raised in St. Bernard Parish, Louisiana, Puddin' Taine traces her love of drag back to the age of three, when she became entranced with the sparkles and feathers of her cousin's dance costumes. When she sought to find her own drag name, it came by way of a childhood memory. When the eccentric, chain-smoking dog groomer known as Puddin' would drop by in her Winnebago, her mother would recite, "Puddin' Taine, Puddin' Taine, ask me again and I'll tell you the same." And the rest is history.

Puddin' traded one fishing village for another, taking the drag scene of Provincetown, Massachusetts, by storm while modestly describing herself as just "a young lady in search of lobster and clam chowder."

In 2018, Puddin' Taine was named Provincetown's Show Girl of the Year, portraying "Popcorn by Hot Butter." With a dress crafted entirely of tin foil, she sported breasts of Jiffy Pop, and a fully functioning popcorn maker served as her chapeau. She returned home victorious to reign as the 2019 queen of Armeinius in the 51st celebration of New Orleans' most lavish and satirical gay Carnival ball.

Puddin' Taine says the secret to great drag is that "the audience has to laugh, has to cry . . . You have to make them feel something real."

Tart à la Bouille

Tableau

Serves 8

This Cajun Country favorite has become a sensation at
Dickie Brennan's Tableau restaurant on Jackson Square.

Crust

1 cup sugar

4 tablespoons unsalted butter,
room temperature

2 eggs

1 teaspoon vanilla extract

2 cups all-purpose flour

1½ teaspoons baking powder

Custard

4 cups milk

2 cups cream

2 eggs

1 cup sugar

¼ teaspoon salt

½ cup cornstarch

2 gelatin sheets

2 cups ice water

2 tablespoons vanilla extract

8 tablespoons unsalted butter

Crust

With an electric mixer, beat together sugar and butter until light and fluffy.
Add eggs one at a time, beating well after each addition. Add vanilla and
mix. In a separate bowl, whisk together flour and baking powder. Add dry
ingredients to wet ingredients and beat for 5 minutes. Form dough into a
ball and wrap in plastic. Chill for 20-30 minutes.

Custard

In a large saucepan over medium heat, bring milk and cream to a low boil.
Combine eggs, sugar, salt, and cornstarch in a bowl. Slowly whisk hot milk
into egg mixture. Transfer to saucepan and cook over low heat, stirring
constantly until it reaches a thick ribbon stage.

Meanwhile, soak gelatin in ice water for 10 minutes. Gently wring out water
and add gelatin to custard, whisking until melted. Remove from heat and
add vanilla extract and butter. Whisk to combine. Cover with plastic wrap.
(Plastic wrap should touch the surface of the cream to avoid the formation
of skin.) Refrigerate, stirring occasionally for even cooling.

Grease and flour a 9-inch pie pan. Roll out dough so that it fits in pan with
½ inch hanging over the edge. Fill pan with cooled custard then fold crust
over the edge. Chill for 30 minutes.

Preheat oven to 325 degrees. Bake for 1 hour, turning pie every 15 minutes
for even baking. Allow to cool, then top with Spiced Rum Caramel.

Spiced Rum Caramel

Yields 2½ cups

¼ cup sugar

¼ cup water

1 cup + 1 tablespoon cream

2 tablespoons spiced rum

1 teaspoon vanilla extract

2 teaspoons chilled, unsalted butter

In a heavy saucepot, combine sugar and water. Cook over high heat until
sugar dissolves and turns an amber color. Remove from heat and slowly
whisk in cream. Return to the stove and cook over a medium heat until
thick, approximately 10 minutes, stirring occasionally. Remove from heat
and stir in spiced rum, vanilla, and butter. Cool before using to sauce.

Creole Crawfish Strudel

Commander's Palace

Chef Tory McPhail

Serves 4

A fresh, crisp salad is the perfect foil for this rich, elegant crawfish strudel.

1 teaspoon oil

1 teaspoon minced garlic

1 large onion, diced

1 large green bell pepper, diced

2 ribs celery, diced

1 pound cremini mushrooms, sliced and roasted

1 large tomato, concassed and diced

1 pound crawfish tails

1 teaspoon chopped fresh tarragon

½ teaspoon chopped fresh thyme

1 teaspoon Creole seasoning

Salt and pepper to taste

4 ounces pepper Jack cheese, diced

1 (12 ounce) sheet puff pastry

1 cup heavy cream, reduced by half

1 red pepper, charred, skin and seeds removed

Salt and pepper to taste

Salad

2 cups mixed greens

1 cup julienned mirliton

½ pint cherry tomatoes, halved

4 ounces haricot verts, cleaned and blanched

1 teaspoon cane vinegar

Salt and pepper to taste

Preheat oven to 400 degrees. Heat oil in a skillet over medium heat. Add garlic and toast for 15 seconds. Mix in onion, bell pepper, and celery; sauté until translucent. Add mushrooms, tomato, crawfish, tarragon, and thyme. Season with Creole seasoning, salt, and pepper. Stir in cheese then immediately remove from heat. Cheese should not be completely melted. Cool mixture in refrigerator.

Spread three-quarters of chilled filling along the long side of puff pastry, leaving 1 inch from edge to seal. Egg wash sides of pastry and fold over filling. Crimp with a fork to seal. Bake for 15 minutes.

Meanwhile, combine reduced cream and charred peppers in a blender. Purée until smooth and season to taste.

Combine all salad ingredients in a bowl. Season to taste and divide among 4 serving plates.

Trim off ends of baked strudel and cut into 4 portions. Serve with salad and top with heated reserved filling and cream.

Irish Channel Stout
Ice Cream Float

Serves 1

There is virtually nothing that this rich, filling breakfast drink can't cure.

1 pint Irish Channel Stout

1 scoop vanilla or chocolate ice cream

Scoop the ice cream into a tall glass. Slowly pour in the stout, stir, and sip.

Auda Beaux Di

Living your best life on stage.

This tongue-twister of a beautiful drag queen began her drag career right out of high school with a performance at a benefit for the Kaleidoscope Youth Center, a special place for LGBTQ teens in Columbus, Ohio.

Auda's drag name springs from a fascination with psychic phenomena, combined with a nod to her Louisiana Creole and French heritage, resulting in a delightful play on words.

Now at home in New Orleans, everything in day-to-day life inspires her. Even when misfortune stumbles in, it often translates into a musical performance. She enthuses, "What's missing in your life is what your drag becomes."

When it comes to drag, for the inspirational Auda, it's simply "living your best life on stage."

Eggs Sardou

Jules Alciatore
Antoine's Restaurant
Serves 4

Jules Alciatore served this dish at a special late-night breakfast honoring Sarah Bernhardt, who was accompanied by 19th-century playwright Victorien Sardou. Although Jules intended to name his creation for the Divine Sarah, she insisted that the honor was due to Sardou because of the plays he created especially for her. Over time, creamed spinach became an accepted part of the dish, but this version is the original.

16 anchovy fillets
8 warmed artichoke bottoms
8 hot poached eggs (see page 61)
2 cups Antoine's Hollandaise Sauce
   (recipe follows)
4 tablespoons chopped ham
8 truffle slices

Cross 2 anchovy fillets across each artichoke bottom. Top with 1 poached egg. Pour ¼ cup hollandaise sauce over each poached egg. Sprinkle with chopped ham and garnish with truffles.

Antoine's Hollandaise Sauce
Yields 2 cups

8 egg yolks
2 tablespoons lemon juice
2 tablespoons tarragon vinegar
2 cups melted butter
¾ teaspoon paprika
Salt and cayenne pepper to taste

Beat egg yolks together with lemon juice and vinegar. Pour into the top of a double boiler. Stirring constantly, cook on a low heat over simmering water, never letting the water come to a boil. Continue cooking until the mixture thickens. Remove from the heat and beat in the melted butter a little at a time. Add the paprika, salt, and pepper. Keep warm.

Sweet Potato Bread

Gracious Bakery

Yields 1 loaf

This is a perfect brunch solution for leftover baked sweet potatoes, and the streusel topping makes this sweet, quick bread a favorite.

2 sweet potatoes

1¾ cups + 2 tablespoons all purpose flour

½ tablespoon baking soda

½ teaspoon baking powder

½ teaspoon cinnamon

½ teaspoon ginger

¼ teaspoon nutmeg

¼ teaspoon allspice

½ teaspoon salt

1¼ cups + 2 tablespoons dark brown sugar

4 tablespoons butter, room temperature

2 eggs

⅓ cup buttermilk

Streusel

⅓ cup all purpose flour

¼ cup light brown sugar

¼ teaspoon cinnamon

Pinch of salt

¼ cup chopped pecans

¼ cup melted butter

Wash sweet potatoes and wrap in aluminum foil. Bake at 375 degrees for 1 hour. Remove from oven and allow to cool. When cool, peel and set aside.

In a bowl, combine flour, baking soda, baking powder, cinnamon, ginger, nutmeg, allspice, and salt. Mix well.

In a stand mixer with a paddle, cream together butter and brown sugar. Add baked sweet potato and mix until combined. Add eggs one at a time. Take turns adding dry ingredients and buttermilk into egg mixture, mixing until thoroughly combined. Pour the batter into a greased loaf pan.

Prepare the streusel by combining all dry ingredients. Add melted butter, combining to create a crumbly texture. Top sweet potato batter with streusel.

Bake at 350 degrees for 1 hour, or until a toothpick inserted into the middle comes out clean. Turn out onto a wire rack and cool for 20 minutes before serving.

Alice's Spoonbread

Chef Susan Spicer

Serves 8

You won't find this dish at any of Chef Susan Spicer's three New Orleans restaurants, Bayona, Mondo, or Rosedale. This simple spoonbread recipe is a childhood favorite coming straight from Susan Spicer's mother, Alice.

¼ cup breadcrumbs
½ cup butter
1 cup finely chopped onion
1 quart milk
1 teaspoon salt
1 cup cornmeal
½ cup white cheddar cheese
Black pepper to taste
4 large egg whites

Preheat oven to 375 degrees. Butter a 2 quart soufflé dish or 8 individual, 8 ounce ramekins, then coat lightly with breadcrumbs, shaking out the excess.

In a 2 quart sauce pot over medium-high heat, melt ¼ cup butter and add the onions. Sauté until onions start to turn a light golden brown. Slowly stir in milk and add salt. Increase heat to medium-high and whisk in cornmeal. Bring to a boil, then reduce heat to low and cook for about 10 minutes, until mixture is very thick, stirring constantly. Remove from heat and stir in the remaining butter, all the cheese, and pepper to taste; let sit for a few minutes to cool. Whip egg whites until they are stiff but not dry, then fold into cornmeal mixture, one-third at a time. Scrape into prepared dish or ramekins and bake until bread is set in the middle (approximately 40 minutes for large dish or 15 minutes for ramekins).

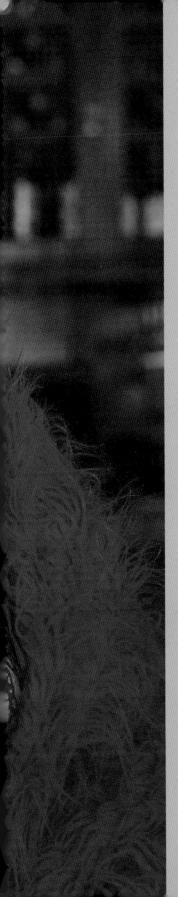

Sunshine Edae

Sunshine can always sunburn

To Sunshine Edae, sunshine means radiance and true self. She first began playing female characters with the Boys of BEARlesque, a New York City "drag-lesque" troupe she remembers as "fat, hairy gay men."

Drag has allowed Sunshine to embody both male and female at the same time. She believes, "There is no line. We're all just made of energy that passes back and forth in the world—just like sunshine itself."

With an esthetic she describes as "like Divine and the Spice Girls had an orgy baby," Sunshine Edae finds eyelashes to be the hardest part of the physical transformation. But her most important preparation before performing is "to be sure my psyche is together. Then, I can tap freely into who I am and feed off of the energy of the crowd. Performing is a message that reflects our times. It allows me to reach humanity and evoke emotions that make a difference."

But be warned! With all of the sweetness and light that Sunshine Edae portrays when performing, she warns, "Don't forget: Sunshine can always sunburn!"

Poppy's IV

Toups' Meatery

Serves 1

I was particularly relieved to learn that this deep crimson cocktail was named in honor of Isaac and Amanda Toups' daughters, Poppy and Ivy, and not intended to be a direct infusion Larry Ngyuen had waiting at the bar for me!

2 ounces gin

1 ounce pickled beet juice

1 ounce Domaine de Canton liquor

2 dashes saline

Pickled beet for garnish

Stir ingredients over ice and strain into chilled coupe. Garnish with a pickled beet.

Fried Louisiana Oyster & Pork Belly BLT

Chef Brian Landry

Jack Rose

Serves 4

Inside the historic Pontchartrain Hotel, brunch at Jack Rose is like taking a wild, irreverent romp through your eccentric great-aunt's St. Charles Avenue mansion.

1 pound cured pork belly

Canola oil for frying

3 cups all purpose flour

2 cups yellow cornmeal

1 cup cornstarch

2 tablespoons Creole seasoning

4 egg whites

12 Louisiana oysters

Salt to taste

8 slices Texas toast

Spicy mayo (½ cup mayonnaise +
   1 tablespoon hot sauce)

2 cups butter lettuce leaves

2 large Creole tomatoes, sliced ¼ inch thick

Slice pork belly into ½-inch-thick strips, each about 4 inches long. Sear the pork belly in a skillet over medium-high heat until browned, then flip and repeat.

In a fryer, heat canola oil to 350 degrees. In a shallow bowl, combine flour, cornmeal, cornstarch, and Creole seasoning. In a separate bowl, beat egg whites. Toss oysters in the whites to coat, then dredge oysters in cornmeal mixture. Fry oysters in oil until golden brown. Drain on paper towels and season lightly with salt.

To assemble the sandwich, toast and lightly butter 2 pieces of Texas toast, then spread with spicy mayo. Place butter lettuce and Creole tomatoes on toast. Top with sliced pork belly, 3 fried oysters, and a piece of toast.

Nevaeh Gates

Wigs, costumes, and rhinestones—it's a lot of work!

Nevaeh Gates turns heaven upside down when she performs in drag, singing worship songs she learned at her Pentecostal church in the Bayou Country of Houma, Louisiana. Nevaeh, a perfect size 6, looks like a piece of heaven as she strums the guitar while singing her original version of "Amazing Grace, Amazing Love."

"The first time I dressed in drag, I felt more myself than ever before," explains Nevaeh. "It was a mind-opening experience. The best part of the transformation is the camaraderie I find among the other drag queens."

Nevaeh's husband is well-known pageant queen Starr Alexander. The downfall to that? "Two drag queens getting ready for a show—packing wigs, sparkling costumes, and all those rhinestones—it's a lot of work!"

Hooch Punch

SoBou

Makes enough punch for a wild party of 18!

Served from a flask, this hooch punch brings the crowd to a roar when Bella Blue and her burlesque dancers perform on Sundays at SoBou. Anything goes when it's served at a Drag Queen Brunch!

4 cups chamomile tea

2 ruby red grapefruits, juiced, zest reserved in wide strips

3 oranges, juiced, zest reserved in wide strips

½ cup fresh lemon juice

3 ounces oleo saccharum (recipe follows)

2 ounces peach bitters

1 liter pineapple rum

1 liter coconut rum

Candied citrus peel for garnish

Mix together first 8 ingredients and pour over ice. Garnish with candied citrus peel.

Oleo Saccharum

Yields about 1 cup

3 oranges, zested

2 grapefruits, zested

1 cup sugar

Zest all citrus fruit in wide strips before juicing. Cover zest in sugar and let sit for several hours or overnight until a syrup forms. The sugar will extract the natural oils and create a pure syrup. Strain off syrup and store in refrigerator.

After extracting the oils, dehydrate the zest to candy them. You can achieve this by using a dehydrator or placing them in the oven at a low heat for 2 hours or more until crisply dried.

Cinnamon Cream Cheese Rolls

Chef Tariq Hanna

Yields 1 dozen

During Mardi Gras, Chef Tariq transforms these same ingredients into his standout king cake recipe!

Dough

⅔ cup milk

⅓ cup sugar

1½ teaspoons yeast

2 eggs

3½ cups bread flour

1 teaspoon kosher salt

1 tablespoon vanilla extract

1 cup unsalted butter

Cinnamon Sugar

8 tablespoons butter, melted

2 cups light brown sugar

2 tablespoons cinnamon

Cream Cheese Filling

1 pound cream cheese

1 egg

1 egg yolk

¼ cup sugar

1 tablespoon vanilla extract

In a stand mixer with a dough hook attachment, combine all the dough ingredients except butter. Mix for about 3 minutes, until strands of gluten are formed. Add in butter and mix 3-4 minutes. Cover and refrigerate at least 2 hours, preferably overnight.

Blend together cinnamon sugar ingredients and reserve.

Combine all cream cheese filling ingredients and cream together well.

On a well-floured surface, roll dough out into an even rectangle. Spread cinnamon sugar mix evenly across the surface. Roll dough into a log of approximately 2 inches in diameter. Cut into 1½-inch slices. Arrange rolls 1 inch apart on lined baking sheet. Coat top of each roll with cream cheese filling. Cover with plastic wrap and let rise until doubled in size.

Preheat oven to 350 degrees. Bake for 12-15 minutes, or until bottom of rolls turns a light golden brown.

(Courtesy Sally Asher)

Piggies in a Blankie

Chef Isaac Toups

Toups' Meatery

Yields 24 Piggies

Sausage

4 pounds ground pork

2 tablespoons freshly grated ginger

½ tablespoon dried oregano

1 tablespoon dried basil

½ tablespoon aleppo pepper

2 tablespoons dark brown sugar

1½ tablespoons kosher salt

Remaining Ingredients

24 ounces frozen puff pastry dough

1½ cups grated cheddar cheese

1 egg, beaten

½ cup Dijon mustard

Mix all sausage ingredients together. Measure 2 tablespoons of sausage mixture and roll into links 3 inches in length and approximately ½ inch thick.

Cut puff pastry into 2x4 inch rectangles. Place 1 teaspoon grated cheese on each piece of puff pastry and top with sausage link. Roll pastry around sausage and seal edge with beaten egg.

Bake at 350 degrees for 10-12 minutes, or until golden brown. Serve with Dijon mustard for dipping.

Boudin Breakfast Burritos

Boudin Breakfast Burritos

Chef Isaac Toups
Toups South
Serves 4

Isaac Toups' boudin is a three-day process, but you can easily buy boudin by the link.

8 boudin links
½ cup sliced pickled jalapeños
   (recipe follows)
8 (8 inch) flour tortillas
½ cup grated white cheddar cheese
1½ cups Tabasco Hollandaise
   (see page 101)

Preheat oven to 350 degrees. Remove boudin from casing. Place boudin filling in a tortilla and top with 1 tablespoon Pickled Jalapeños and 1 tablespoon cheese. Wrap tightly and brown on both sides in a cast-iron skillet over high heat, pressing down slightly to flatten. Bake for 12-15 minutes. Serve with Tabasco Hollandaise.

There's nothing like Isaac's Pickled Jalapeños! Once the peppers have been eaten, Isaac and his crew love to knock back a whiskey shot with a good pickleback chaser.

If you have never sliced fresh jalapeños, *stop right here!* Wear gloves when handling the hot peppers. A thick coating of cooking oil rubbed onto your hands will also protect your skin. Be forewarned, you do not want to touch any delicate body parts after getting jalapeños on your hands!

Pickled Jalapeños

Makes 1 quart

1 quart jalapeños, sliced
1¼ cups white wine vinegar
½ cup sugar
2 tablespoons honey
1 teaspoon ground black pepper
1 bay leaf
¼ teaspoon
Salt

Soak sliced jalapeños in 5 cups of ice cold water. Agitate gently and skim off any seeds that rise to the top. Leave remaining seeds. Drain well then transfer pepper slices to a quart Mason jar.

Combine remaining ingredients with ¾ cups water in a non-reactive (stainless steel or tin) pot. Bring to a boil then reduce heat to low. Simmer uncovered for 20 minutes. Pour hot liquid over jalapeños in Mason jar. Cool to room temperature then cover and refrigerate. Keep refrigerated for up to 1 month.

Pickleback Shot

Serves 1

Be warned, Drag Queens may feel faint from the effects.

3 ounces whiskey
3 ounces jalapeño pickle juice

Pour whiskey and jalapeño pickle juice into separate jiggers. Shoot the whiskey then chase it with the jigger of juice.

Tabasco Hollandaise

Chef Isaac Toups

Toups South

Yields 1 cup

Isaac's hollandaise sauce is spicy enough to stand up to any Cajun dish.

2 egg yolks

1 teaspoon Tabasco

2 teaspoons Dijon mustard

8 tablespoons butter, melted

1 lemon, juiced

Kosher salt to taste

In a medium-sized metal mixing bowl, combine egg yolks, Tabasco, and Dijon mustard.

Fill a medium skillet with ½ inch of water. Bring to a simmer over medium heat. Place metal bowl with egg mixture in the water and whisk immediately. Continue whisking, turning bowl as you go, until thick ribbons form.

Remove bowl from heat and drizzle in butter in a slow stream, whisking continuously to make sure butter is fully emulsified. Whisk in lemon juice and salt to taste.

Hollandaise Sauce

Brennan's

Yields 2 cups

A classic hollandaise to dress up any brunch dish.

8 egg yolks

4 tablespoons lemon juice

1 pound butter, melted

½ teaspoon salt

⅛ teaspoon pepper

In the top half of double boiler over low heat, beat egg yolks and lemon juice together. Whisking constantly, cook very slowly, never allowing water in bottom of pan to come to a boil. Add butter a little at a time, stirring constantly with a wooden spoon. Add salt and pepper. Continue cooking slowly until thickened.

Mrs. Holly N. Dazed

Salty, delicious, and full of fat!

When comparing herself to the hollandaise sauce that inspired her name, this buxom beauty of a chef-ette proclaims, "I'm just like the sauce: salty, delicious, and full of fat!"

Having grown up in Thibodaux, Louisiana, surrounded by football-loving, beer-drinking, women-chasing He-Men, Holly found that her 2017 move to New Orleans changed her life. There she discovered the art form of drag, which allowed her to explore her feminine side.

Broadway glitz and glamour inspires her big wigs and even bigger personality. She revels in the fun, camp, and theatrics of drag. The one-time bayou boy warns, however, "You have to be brave to put on heels, wigs, and eyelashes!"

For Mrs. Holly N. Dazed, sauciness is not just a brunch option anymore, it's everyday life.

Strawberry Sparkler

Lu Brow
Brennan's
Serves 1

At the classic pink building on Royal Street, master bar chef Lu Brow creates a perfect, strawberry pink drink with a meticulous eye for fresh, local ingredients.

2 ounces chilled strawberry basil
   syrup (recipe follows)
3-4 ounces champagne or sparkling wine
Basil leaf for garnish

Pour 2 ounces strawberry basil syrup into a cocktail coupe. Add champagne or sparkling wine to fill and garnish with a basil leaf.

Strawberry Basil Syrup

Yields approximately 2 cups

1 pint Louisiana strawberries, quartered
¼ cup granulated sugar
1 cup very hot water
½ cup fresh basil leaves

Muddle strawberries with sugar until sugar is saturated with juice. Add water and basil and allow the mixture to steep for 20 minutes. Stir the mixture and strain until the juice is free of seeds. Refrigerate mixture for up to 1 week.

Eggs Hussarde

Brennan's

Serves 4

In the 1950s, Brennan's founder, Owen Brennan, Sr., would order Eggs Benedict from Chef Paul Blange then ladle a spoonful of marchands de vin over the hollandaise sauce. Inspired by the combination of flavors, Blange created Eggs Hussarde, naming the dish after the brave Prussian military men of the Napoleonic Wars who were said to only eat meat. It remains a favorite at Brennan's today.

8 thin slices ham, grilled

8 Holland rusks

2 cups marchands de vin (recipe follows)

1 large tomato, cut into 8 slices and grilled

8 soft poached eggs (see page 61)

2 cups Hollandaise Sauce (see page 101)

Paprika for garnish

Lay a large slice of ham across each rusk and top with marchands de vin. Top with tomato slice and 1 egg. Spoon hollandaise Sauce over each serving. Garnish with sprinkling of paprika.

Marchands de Vin

Yields 2 cups

6 tablespoons butter

6 tablespoons finely chopped mushrooms

¼ cup minced ham

4 tablespoons finely chopped shallots

¼ cup finely chopped onion

1 tablespoon minced garlic

1 tablespoon flour

½ teaspoon salt

⅛ teaspoon black pepper

Dash cayenne

½ cup beef stock

¼ cup red wine

In a 9-inch skillet over medium-high heat, melt butter and lightly sauté the mushrooms, ham, shallots, onion, and garlic. When the onion is golden brown, add the flour, salt, black pepper, and cayenne. Brown well, about 7-10 minutes. Blend in the stock and the wine and simmer over low heat for 35-45 minutes until thickened.

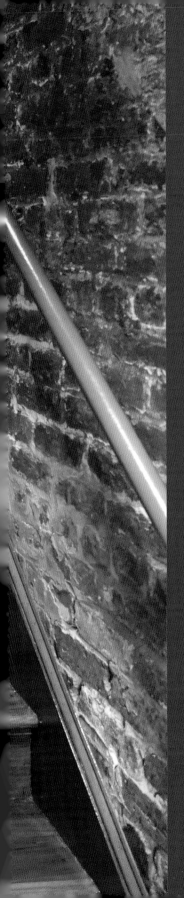

Princesse Stephaney

Anything for a gag and a dollar.

Princesse Stephaney's storied drag career began at a political fundraiser in 2002, when an old glamour queen revealed she had just made $350 for her performance, to which the soon-to-be princess responded, "Book me!"

When performing in Memphis in the 1980s, she wore fluorescent green shorts and a pink tank top while sporting a long, dark wig. Audiences took one look at her and proclaimed, "It's Princess Stephaney!" As there was already a Princess Stephanie in each of the European monarchies of Belgium, Monaco, and the Netherlands, she became Princesse Stephaney de la Nouvelle-Orléans.

From the start, Princesse Stephaney's motto has been "Anything for a gag and a dollar." True to form, she has worn blowup dolls on stage and perfected an act that involves a small dog escaping from a huge hoop skirt.

When Princesse Stephaney performs, she often fights a battle between singing a song to make a buck and singing a song simply for herself. There's never a dry eye in the house when she gives her rendition of "Playing Barbie" by Pink.

After decades onstage, the Princesse gives back to the LGBTQ community, often performing for charity events. Princesse Stephaney is the only drag queen to serve as an official, sanctioned Louisiana festival queen. She reigned as Mirliton Queen 2003, and jaws dropped when her photo appeared in a national airline magazine, urging travelers to "Go to the Festival and Meet the Queen!"

If the queen is Princesse Stephaney, you won't be disappointed!

Barbeque Shrimp & Cream Cheese Grits

Chef Chip Flanagan
Ralph's on the Park
Serves 4

Shrimp and grits originally hails from the Carolinas, but Chef Chip Flanagan makes a distinctly New Orleans version with delicious barbeque shrimp.

24 large shrimp, head on
4 tablespoons Worcestershire sauce
3 tablespoons coarsely ground black pepper
1 tablespoon Creole seasoning
4 cloves garlic, minced
1 lemon, seeded
½ pound chilled unsalted butter, cut into 24 tablespoon-sized chunks

Place unpeeled shrimp, Worcestershire sauce, black pepper, Creole seasoning, garlic, and 1 tablespoon of water in a heavy 10-inch, stainless-steel sauté pan. Squeeze lemon juice over shrimp then add lemon rind and pulp to the pan. Over high heat, cook shrimp for about 2 minutes, gently stirring and turning shrimp until partially cooked. Reduce heat to medium-high and gradually stir the cold pieces of butter into the pan until they are incorporated into the pan juices and the sauce is light brown and creamy. Turn the shrimp occasionally in the sauce.

Divide shrimp and serve atop Cream Cheese Grits. Strain the butter sauce and pour over each serving.

Cream Cheese Grits

Yields 4 cups

¾ cup stone ground grits
2 cups chicken stock
¾ cup heavy cream
6½ tablespoons cream cheese
Salt and pepper to taste
3 tablespoons Parmesan cheese

Combine the grits, chicken stock, heavy cream, salt, and pepper in a pot. Bring to a boil then reduce to a slow simmer. Stir the grits frequently to prevent sticking and burning. If the grits get too thick, add water as necessary and continue stirring. When grits are cooked, stir in cream cheese and Parmesan cheese. Season with additional salt and pepper to taste.

Tasso Baked Eggs

Chef Jarred Zeringue

EAT New Orleans

Serves 4

For a fabulous presentation, take the bubbling cast-iron skillet right to the table. Everyone will want to dig right in with warm French bread toast.

¼ cup Italian breadcrumbs

8 tablespoons butter, melted, divided

1 cup diced tasso

3 green onions sliced

3 tablespoons chopped Italian parsley

2 teaspoons salt

2 teaspoons black pepper

¼ teaspoon thyme

1 cup heavy cream

8 eggs

1 loaf French bread, sliced, buttered, and toasted

Preheat oven broiler. In a small bowl, combine breadcrumbs with 2 tablespoons butter; set aside.

In a cast-iron skillet over medium-high heat, sauté diced tasso in remaining butter with green onions, parsley, salt, and black pepper until lightly browned. Add heavy cream and when large bubbles form, crack in eggs one at a time. Remove from heat and top with breadcrumb mixture.

Place the skillet under the broiler until egg whites set. Remove from oven and let cool slightly. Meanwhile, place buttered French bread under broiler.

To eat, dip French bread in the yolks and tasso cream.

Starr Alexander

Polished, pretty, prim, and proper.

For pageant queen Starr Alexander, drag is all about the glitz and glam, the rhinestones, and the evening gowns. She grew up watching Miss America and playing with her Barbie dolls. "I wanted to be just like Barbie," Starr says, "polished, pretty, prim, and proper."

She's outdone Barbie herself, winning Miss Gay Louisiana USofA, Miss Gay Vieux Carré America, Miss New Orleans Pride, Miss AIDS Awareness, Miss Golden Lantern, and Miss Gay Bolt America. That's quite an accomplishment for a girl from Denham Springs, Louisiana, where she lived for an entire year in drag before she began performing.

It wasn't easy for her devoutly Southern Baptist grandmother, who would highlight verses in the Bible especially for Starr. But now, both her mother and grandmother frequently catch her on stage performing "Amazing Grace" as Dolly Parton.

The buxom, beautiful Starr—a dead ringer for Adele—used her likeness to the singer to capture the Miss Gay Louisiana title. Starr's version introduced an Adele that audiences had never seen before, complete with backup dancers, a bounce remix, and a rip-away skirt.

A performance by the one and only Starr Alexander is a treat not to be missed!

Cracklin' Biscuits

Chef Jarred Zeringue

Wayne Jacob's Smokehouse and Restaurant

Yields 24 biscuits

There's nothing to compare with fresh, hot cracklin's right out of the pot at Wayne Jacob's Smokehouse. If you can spare 2 cups of the goodies, the biscuits that Chef Jarred Zeringue's mom makes are out of this world. Especially when slathered with cane syrup butter!

2½ cups Pioneer biscuit mix
½ cup sour cream
6 ounces Abita Amber beer
1 cup chopped cracklin's

Preheat oven to 350 degrees. Mix all ingredients together and drop by tablespoonfuls onto baking sheet. Bake for 20-25 minutes until lightly browned. Serve with lots of cane syrup butter.

Cane Syrup Butter

Yields 1 cup

2 sticks butter, room temperature
½ cup cane syrup

Cream together in mixer and chill.

Whiskey Punch

Tujague's Restaurant

Serves 1

Philip Guichet won first place in the Early Times National Cocktail Mixed Drink Competition in 1956 with this creamy breakfast cocktail. A punch bowl filled with this creamy, high-proof drink is a Drag Queen Brunch waiting to happen!

2 ounces bourbon whiskey

1 whole egg

2 ounces pure cream

4 drops orange flower water

2 teaspoons sugar

Grated nutmeg

Combine all ingredients in a cocktail shaker over crushed ice. Shake vigorously for 2-3 minutes then strain into a stemmed cocktail glass. Garnish with grated nutmeg.

(Courtesy Sally Asher)

Lana O'Day

Dancer, singer, model, and so much more

Standing in line to see a movie, Lana received an urgent text: "I need your drag name. We're printing the posters for the show!" Raised by a movie-loving grandmother, Lana grew up with an old Hollywood aesthetic. Deciding on Lana Turner's first name, she quickly flipped through her numbers and settled on singer Aubrey O'Day's surname for her last.

A late bloomer, Lana saw her first drag show on her first date as a gay man and was completely entranced by the beauty. Her whole life she'd wanted to be a dancer, a singer, a model—but wasn't good at any of those things. As a drag queen, Lana found she could be all those things and so much more.

Lana loves traditional drag rooted in pageant and glamour, but at Halloween she often grows a full beard, becoming an alternate queen she calls Rock Hunter O'Day. That beard is the perfect accessory when she dresses as Snow White while performing the favorites "Whistle While You Twerk" and "Talk Dirty to the Animals."

Drag has profoundly changed Lana's life. Pushed to be out in such a vulnerable way has become an exhilarating liberation. Lana O'Day says her greatest freedom came with being able to marry her husband in November 2018.

Red Bean & XO Salad with Roasted Pork Belly & Crispy Sticky Rice Cakes

Chef Michael Gulotta

MoPho

Serves 6

These aren't your mama's red beans! Chef Michael Gulotta gives a New Orleans standard a decidedly Asian twist.

Red Bean Salad

3 cups cooked red beans, drained
   (recipe follows)

2 shallots, minced

1-inch finger fresh ginger, minced

2 tablespoons XO sauce

1 tablespoon seasoned rice wine vinegar

1 cup finely chopped cilantro

½ jalapeño, deseeded and finely chopped

Fish sauce to taste

6 poached eggs, optional (see page 61)

Combine all ingredients in a small saucepan over medium heat, but do not boil.

To serve, place ½ cup red bean salad on plate and top with 4 slices of warmed pork belly and 3 cubes of crispy rice cakes. For Drag Queen Brunch deliciousness, add a poached egg to each serving.

Red Beans

6 ounces smoked pork, diced

1 onion, small diced

1 green bell pepper, small diced

5 cloves garlic, crushed

1 small finger of ginger, minced

1 stalk lemongrass, crushed

1 stalk celery, small diced

1 quart dried red beans, soaked in cold water
overnight

3 tablespoons smoked paprika

1 teaspoon cayenne

1 bay leaf

Salt to taste

In a large pot, render pork over medium-high heat until it is golden brown. Add onion, pepper, garlic, ginger, lemongrass, and celery to the pot and sauté until translucent. Add the remaining ingredients and enough water to cover beans by 1 inch. Bring to a boil then reduce to a simmer. Simmer for no more than 2 hours. Beans should be tender but not mushy. Add salt to taste and allow beans to cool in their liquid.

Pork Belly

¼ cup kosher salt

½ cup sugar

½ teaspoon crushed red pepper

2 pounds pork belly

1 onion, cut into ½ inch slices

1 head garlic, split and broken into cloves

Mix together salt, sugar, and crushed red pepper. Evenly coat the pork belly and refrigerate overnight.

Preheat oven to 325 degrees. In a deep baking pan, arrange onions and halved garlic cloves. Place the pork belly on top. Fill the pan with water until halfway up the pork belly. Roast uncovered for 50 minutes. Increase the heat to 425 degrees and roast for an additional 20 minutes. Remove pork from the oven and allow to cool in the remaining broth until warm. Transfer the pork to a cutting board and cut into 2-inch-thick slices.

Sticky Rice Cakes

3 cups glutinous white rice, rinsed under
cool running water for 10 minutes.

16 ounces canned coconut water

2-inch finger fresh ginger, sliced in half

1 stalk lemongrass, split

1 tablespoon salt

½ cup seasoned rice wine vinegar

2 cups sliced green onions

1 cup rice flour

½ cup vegetable oil

Combine rice, 3 cups water, coconut water, ginger, lemongrass, and salt in a rice cooker. Cook according to directions. Toss cooked rice with seasoned rice wine vinegar and green onions. Spread evenly on a parchment-lined baking sheet and allow to cool. Once cool, cut cakes into 1-inch cubes. Dip knife in hot water between slices to prevent sticking.

Roll the cubes in rice flour. Heat vegetable oil over high heat in a skillet and brown rice cakes on both sides. Drain on paper towel and salt lightly. Keep warm until ready to serve.

Cucci Licci
Crazy Rich Asian

Cucci Licci's first venture into drag was in her senior year at Isidore Newman School. The self-described "quiet, nerdy choir kid" showed up for school on Halloween in a Lady Gaga-esque white crystal gown, turning some heads in the process.

Musical studies at Loyola University delayed Cucci's drag dreams, but now the winsome Asian beauty explores her extreme feminine side on stage while performing in her sister's best sundress. "I helped her pick it out, but once we got home, the dress fit me too and was perfect for my 'Crazy Rich Asian' brunch number," she exclaims.

Sporting a tight Sailor Moon T-shirt with glittery, rose gold platform Lolita boots from Japan, she's a sexy anime character come to life. Always in style, her drag name, Cucci, leaps from Korea's pop music charts, inspired by Jessi's song "Gucci." Hot summer childhood memories of eating ice-cold lychee fruit complete the moniker.

In her gender binary world, Cucci also has a more masculine performance identity she calls Sora, whose original compositions are inspired by K-Pop artists. No matter which act you catch, you won't be disappointed!

(Courtesy Sally Asher)

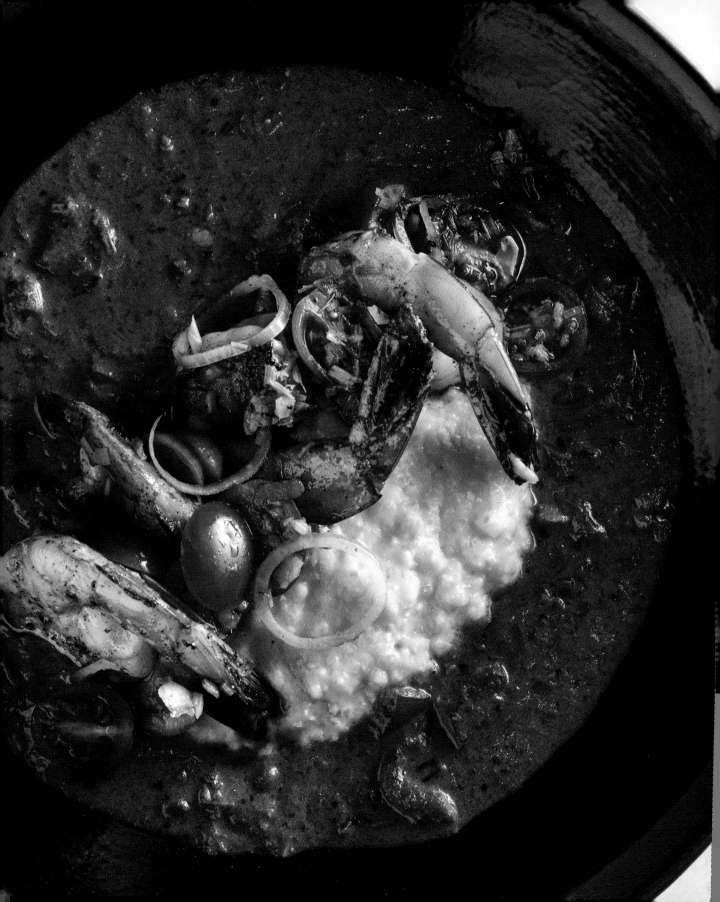

Gulf Shrimp in Smoked Paprika Curry over Grits

Chef Michael Gulotta

Maypop

Serves 6

At Maypop, Chef Michael Gulotta turns the Southern classic, shrimp and grits, upside down with a panoply of Asian flavors.

2 tablespoons virgin coconut oil

1 shallot, minced

3 cloves garlic, minced

2 tablespoons minced fresh ginger

⅓ stalk lemongrass, minced

2 tablespoons shrimp paste

1 tablespoon smoked paprika

2 fresh Thai chilis, sliced (or 1 pinch crushed red pepper flakes)

24 jumbo Gulf shrimp

3 medium ripe tomatoes, diced

2 cups coconut milk

1 lime leaf

½ bunch cilantro, chopped

Fish sauce (or salt) to taste

Fresh lime juice to taste

In a non-reactive pot, heat coconut oil over medium-high heat. Sauté the shallots, garlic, ginger, lemongrass, shrimp paste, smoked paprika, and Thai chilis together until golden brown, about 3 minutes. Add the shrimp and sauté for an additional 3 minutes.

Stir in the tomatoes, coconut milk, and lime leaf, and bring to a simmer. Remove the shrimp from the pan and reserve. Simmer the curry for 5 minutes. Return the shrimp to the pan, stir in the cilantro, and season to taste with fish sauce. Serve over grits.

Grits

Yields 6 cups

1 cup stone ground grits

4 cups water

2 tablespoons butter

½ pound mascarpone cheese

½ cup coconut milk

3 cloves roasted garlic, smashed into a paste

Salt to taste

In a medium pot, bring water to a boil over high heat. Whisk in the grits and continue to stir until the grits begin to thicken, about 3 minutes. Cover the pot and reduce heat to low. Simmer for 20 minutes, stirring occasionally to prevent scorching. Once the grits are tender, remove the pot from the heat and whip in the butter, mascarpone, coconut milk, and roasted garlic. Season with salt to taste.

Shakshouka

Saba

Chef Alon Shaya

Serves 4-6

Chef Alon Shaya brings the flavors of Israel to the Crescent City. With roots in Morocco, Tunisia, and Yemen, this hearty dish showcases the melting pot that is Israeli food.

1 tablespoon + 2 teaspoons kosher salt, divided

½ pound Jerusalem artichokes

1 pound fava beans in their shells

3 tablespoons extra virgin olive oil

1 pint cherry tomatoes, halved

1 small red bell pepper, seeded and thinly sliced

1 small green bell pepper, seeded and thinly sliced

1 small yellow onion, thinly sliced

2 cloves garlic, minced

28 ounces canned peeled whole tomatoes, coarsely chopped

4-6 eggs (1 per serving)

¼ cup zhoug (recipe follows)

In a large pot bring water and 1 tablespoon salt to a boil. Boil Jerusalem artichokes 30-35 minutes, until easily pierced with a knife. Do not overcook. Drain and allow to cool then slice evenly.

Meanwhile, boil fava beans for 5 minutes, or until outer shell puffs and pulls away from the bean. Drain then transfer to a bowl filled with ice water to stop the cooking. When beans are cool, shell them and set aside.

In a large skillet over high heat, sauté cherry tomatoes in olive oil. When tomatoes blister, stir in bell peppers, onion, and garlic. Cook 4 minutes, stirring frequently, until vegetables are golden around the edges and cherry tomatoes break down. Reduce heat to medium and mix in canned tomatoes, Jerusalem artichokes, fava beans, and 2 teaspoons salt. Cook until sauce begins to thicken. Reduce heat to medium-low. Using a spoon, make divots in the sauce, one per egg. Crack an egg into each divot, cover the pan, and cook 4-5 minutes, until egg white is set but the center still jiggles. Dollop a spoonful of zhoug over each egg before serving.

Zhoug

Yields 1 cup

1 clove garlic

3 serrano peppers, halved, seeded, and pith removed

2 cups fresh cilantro leaves

1 cup fresh parsley leaves

½ orange, zested

1 teaspoon kosher salt

½ teaspoon ground cumin

¼ teaspoon ground clove

¼ teaspoon ground cardamom

¼ teaspoon sugar

⅓ cup distilled white vinegar

2 tablespoons extra virgin olive oil

In a food processor, pulse garlic clove. Turn off processor and add serrano peppers, cilantro, and parsley. Pulse together until everything is finely chopped. Add remaining ingredients and pulse together until smooth. Add 1 tablespoon water if needed.

Nectar Ice Cream Soda, Drag Queen Style

Serves 1

The New Orleans flavor known as "nectar" is pink incarnate. Every good New Orleans drag queen enjoyed a nectar snowball or ice cream soda as a child. The addition of vodka makes this a decidedly grown-up soda!

¼ cup Nectar Cream (recipe follows)
2 ounces vodka
Crushed ice
4 ounces seltzer water
Whipped cream
Maraschino cherry

Mix Nectar Cream and vodka together and pour over crushed ice in a tall glass. Top with cold seltzer water. Top with whipped cream and for goodness' sake, don't forget the cherry!

Nectar Cream

Yields 3 cups

3 cups sugar
3 tablespoons clear vanilla
3 tablespoons almond extract
1 cup canned evaporated milk
1 tablespoon red food coloring

Boil sugar and 1 cup water together for 5 minutes. Cool completely. Stir in remaining ingredients. Store refrigerated for up to 2 weeks.

Desirée Josephine Duplantier

Do it right and it will blow up.

Desirée Josephine Duplantier made her first appearance on a Halloween night. The response was so overwhelming that Desirée became a way of life for artist Andrew LaMar Hopkins.

A drag artist from the 1960s and '70s named the lovely apparition Desirée, warning her, "Honey, if you do it right, it will blow up!" and that's just what happened. In a nod to both Josephine Baker and Napoleon Bonaparte's wife, Josephine became her middle name. In tribute to her love for Louisiana history, Duplantier finished her moniker nicely.

Desirée describes herself as a "Creole Mae West, with a classic Coca-Cola bottle shape." No one rocks a Hermès scarf and pearls quite like Desirée, who says, "Desirée is very high maintenance. She's not leaving the house without her pantyhose!" When she makes her entrance at a party, everyone wants to know her. Chateau doors have opened for the beautiful Desirée.

She believes her best attribute is a listening ear. Desirée Josephine Duplantier is an advisor to all who seek her out. Her true purpose is to freely dispense happiness to all.

Courtesy Sally Asher

Rampart Street Stuffed Crabs

Mister Gregory's

Serves 6

Craft cocktail bar Bar Tonique is just next door to Mister Gregory's on Rampart Street. Their Bloody Mary mix gives his stuffed crabs great depth of flavor, while a light finish of bacon grease adds the crowning touch.

1 dozen large fresh blue crabs or 1 pound
   lump crabmeat
3 tablespoons butter
⅓ cup minced green onions, white parts only
⅓ cup minced red bell pepper
⅓ cup minced celery with leaves
1 tablespoon chopped parsley
1 teaspoon Creole mustard
2 eggs, beaten
4 cups finely crushed butter crackers
2½ cups Bar Tonique Bloody Mary Mix
   (recipe follows) or tomato passata
¼ cup bacon grease or butter, melted

Steam and pick crabs. Scrub the top shells and reserve. Refrigerate crabmeat.

Melt butter in a deep skillet. Sauté green onions, red bell pepper, and celery until golden brown. Cool completely.

Preheat oven to 400 degrees. In a bowl, carefully combine cooled seasoning vegetables, crabmeat, parsley, Creole mustard, eggs, and cracker crumbs. Fill shells (or baking dishes) with stuffing. Brush tops with warm bacon grease or butter. Bake for 20 minutes, or until lightly browned.

Mr. Gregory suggests, "Serve with lemon wedges and a strong Bloody Mary made with the remaining mix and bacon-washed vodka, garnished with a crispy piece of bacon."

Bar Tonique Bloody Mary Mix

Bar Tonique

Yields about 6 cups

1 quart strained fresh tomato juice
1½ cups strained fresh lemon juice
1 small onion, juiced
1 jalapeño, juiced
3 cloves garlic, juiced
5 pinches red salt
4 pinches ground black pepper

Combine all ingredients and store refrigerated.

Dirty Boys

Inspired by Chef Frank Brigtsen

Makes 12 sandwiches

What Drag Queen could possibly resist a dirty boy? These sandwiches are long a kitchen favorite at Chef Frank's Riverbend restaurant, Brigtsen's, where all the cooks love to have the dirty-rice meat and seasoning stuffed in a toasted, buttered baguette. Note: Dirty Boys are great at drag queen brunch picnics! Wrapped in shiny aluminum foil, they're delightful to hold and delicious to eat out of hand.

¼ cup oil

½ cup flour

1 onion, chopped

3 stalks celery, chopped

½ bell pepper, chopped

½ pound ground beef

½ pound ground pork

½ pound chicken livers

3 garlic cloves, chopped

1 bay leaf

½ teaspoon salt

⅛ teaspoon cayenne

½ teaspoon coarsely ground
   black pepper

2 tablespoons Worcestershire Sauce

¾ cup beef stock

6 green onions, thinly sliced

1 dozen pistolettes

4 tablespoons butter, melted

Make a roux by combining oil and flour in a large, heavy pot over medium-high heat, stirring continuously until it reaches a milk chocolate brown. Add onion and stir for about 3 minutes, until roux darkens to a bittersweet chocolate brown. Add celery and bell pepper and cook 3-5 minutes, or until translucent.

In a separate pan, brown the ground beef and pork. Strain off all grease and stir meat into roux and seasonings. Chop chicken livers to a fine texture in a food processor. Stir into meat mixture. Add garlic, bay leaf, salt, cayenne, black pepper, Worcestershire sauce, and beef stock, stirring together well. Simmer together for 30 minutes, stirring frequently to avoid sticking. Mix in green onions.

Brush pistolettes with melted butter and bake at 325 degrees for 15 minutes. Split pistolettes in half and fill with meat. Return filled pistolettes to oven and bake for 7-10 minutes, until pistolettes are browned and crunchy.

(Courtesy Sally Asher)

Crêpes Fitzgerald

Brennan's

6 servings (2 crêpes per person)

Named for the Fitzgerald Advertising Agency, which kept a table for 8 reserved at Brennan's Monday through Friday year-round, Crêpes Fitzgerald was originally made exclusively with strawberries. In Brennan's new incarnation, strawberries are reserved for spring, while fresh peaches, blueberries, and other local fruits are flambéed for Fitzgerald during the rest of the year.

Batter

1 cup water
¾ cup milk
½ teaspoon salt
2 teaspoons sugar
3 eggs
1¼ cups flour
5 tablespoons butter, melted

Crêpe Filling

¼ cup cream cheese
1¼ cups sour cream
2 tablespoons sugar
1 teaspoon lemon zest

Fitzgerald Sauce

6 tablespoons butter
6 tablespoons sugar
3 cups sliced strawberries
    or other seasonal fruit
¼ cup kirsch, brandy, or other liqueur

In a mixing bowl, whisk together water, milk, salt, sugar, and eggs. Add flour and mix well. There should be no lumps in the batter. Stir in the melted butter and mix until smooth. Refrigerate batter and allow to rest at least 1 hour before cooking.

Using a hand mixer, beat together cream cheese, sugar, and lemon zest until smooth. Add sour cream and mix until combined. Refrigerate until batter is ready.

Heat an 8-inch non-stick skillet or lightly oiled crêpe pan over medium-high heat. Pour ¼ cup cold crêpe batter onto pan and swirl to spread batter evenly. Cook for 2 minutes, or until browned around the edges. Using a spatula, carefully flip the crêpe and brown on the other side for approximately 25 seconds. Set aside on wax paper. Oil pan and repeat process for each crêpe.

Crêpes may be stacked on top of each other and stored in the refrigerator for up to 2 days.

Fill each crêpe with cream cheese filling and fold in quarters.

In a chafing dish, melt the butter. Add sugar, stirring until sugar dissolves. Add strawberries or other seasonal fruit and cook for 2-3 minutes until slightly softened. Add liqueur and flambé. Serve over warm, filled crêpes.

Savory Pain Perdu

Serves 4

This twist on the classic pain perdu utilizes fresh French bread instead of stale and includes a pocket for stuffing with delicious, savory ingredients.

8 slices fresh French bread, cut 1½ inches thick

8 ounces herbed soft cheese (goat, farmer's, or cream cheese mixed with fresh herbs of choice)

1½ cups milk

6 eggs

1 tablespoon hot sauce

4 tablespoons butter

Without cutting all the way through, cut a pocket into the center of each slice of French bread. Divide the cheese into 8 portions and stuff each slice of bread.

In a bowl, whisk together the milk, eggs, and hot sauce. Briefly soak each piece of stuffed bread in the milk mixture.

Melt butter in a 10-inch skillet and when large bubbles form, add the stuffed French bread pieces, browning lightly on each side.

Serve with chutney or a pickled vegetable relish.

Crab Calas

Yields 18 calas

Savory calas are a modern addition to the Creole food scene. Any savory ingredient can be added to the basic calas mixture.

2 cups cooked rice
6 tablespoons flour
2 teaspoons baking powder
¼ teaspoon salt
½ pound claw crabmeat
3 thinly sliced green onions
2 eggs
1 tablespoon hot sauce
Vegetable oil for deep frying

Thoroughly mix the rice and dry ingredients together with crabmeat and green onions. Add the eggs and hot sauce and mix well.

Heat oil in a deep fryer to 360 degrees. Drop mixture by spoonfuls into oil. Brown calas on one side then turn them to brown the other side. Drain on paper. Serve hot with remoulade sauce for dipping.

Poppy's Remoulade Sauce

Yield 2 cups

Brightly red in color, this spicy remoulade is an authentic rendition of early New Orleans remoulades, when spicy Creole mustard was served in place of the mayonnaise commonly used today.

1 bunch green onions
1 celery heart with tops
½ bunch parsley
1 cup Creole mustard
½ cup olive oil
4 tablespoons paprika
½ teaspoon cayenne
1 teaspoon salt
1 lemon, juiced

Combine green onions, celery, and parsley in food processor. Process until finely minced. Add remainder of the ingredients. Serve as dipping sauce for the savory calas.

(Courtesy Sally Asher)

Pecan Waffle with Cane Syrup

Serves 4

One of my favorite childhood memories involves Camellia Grill's pecan waffle. My personal version, dripping with warmed pecan butter, is even better than I remember from way back then.

Waffle

1½ cups milk

4 tablespoons butter

1 teaspoon vanilla extract

1¾ cups flour

½ cup finely ground pecans

1 teaspoon salt

4 teaspoons baking powder

2 tablespoons sugar

2 eggs

Syrup

4 tablespoons butter

1 cup coarsely chopped pecans

1½ cups dark cane syrup

In a saucepan over medium-high heat, heat the milk and butter together until butter melts. Do not overheat! Stir in vanilla then set aside.

In a large bowl mix together flour, ground pecans, salt, baking powder, and sugar. Mix in eggs then beat milk mixture into flour mixture. Pour half of batter into a waffle maker and cook until done.

In a saucepan, melt butter. Add chopped pecans and cook until pecans are toasted. Add dark cane syrup and mix well.

Serve waffles topped with syrup.

Café Brulot Diabolique

Antoine's Restaurant

Serves 6

What translates as "devilishly burned coffee" was created in the 1880s by Antoine's son, Jules. It was commonplace for diners of the day to flame a sugar cube with cognac before dousing the flame with hot, black coffee. With the addition of citrus and spices, Jules created a masterpiece that remains a tableside showstopper at Antoine's Restaurant today.

2 sticks cinnamon

8 whole cloves

Peel of 1 lemon

1½ tablespoons sugar

3 ounces brandy

3 cups strong black coffee, hot

Put the cinnamon, cloves, lemon peel, sugar, and brandy in a fireproof bowl and heat on an open flame. When the brandy is hot, but not boiling, bring the bowl to the table and ignite with a match. Use a ladle to stir and pour the liquid around the bowl for 2 minutes. Pour hot coffee into the flaming brandy and then ladle into demitasse cups.

Brother Joe Middleton, OFM, discerned his vocation at New Orleans' Tau House during the AIDS crisis in the 1980s. He entered the order of the Sacred Heart Province and lived as a Franciscan until his death in August of 2016.
(*Clarion Ledger\USA TODAY Network*)

EPILOGUE

This book has been a passion project for me, largely inspired by my friendship with Joe Middleton, OFM. Joe and I first met in the late 1970s at the Lee Barnes Cooking School. Joe became my brother, my best friend, and my confidante and he became my favorite playmate. Joe introduced me to his friends, the Demented Women, a wild, rollicking bunch of drag queens often found performing at gay hangouts throughout the French Quarter of the 1980s. Their style of drag always included a gimmick, with every show ending in an ensemble number. Drag for them was all about magic, illusion, beauty—and a whole lot of glitter.

With dubious beginnings at the Golden Lantern as Patty Puke (aka Danny Wilson) and the Regurgitations, the troupe of Demented Women soon grew to include Miss E, Blanche, Mary, Jane, Eunice, Midge, Lurch, S'il Vous Plaît, Alvina Mae, Cakey-T, Olive, Ruby, and Kathleen Conlon—who was born female but still allowed to participate.

Joe relished the role of costume mistress and dresser, inspiring productions such as "Gour-Mae" and "Heels on Wheels." With his culinary career never far behind, he often catered the shows as well.

When Ruby (Robby Hayward) and George Goode formalized their relationship with a wedding (sadly, without municipal blessing), Joe crafted George's wedding dress entirely of paper doilies. The Demented bridesmaids all wore pink lamé, matching Robby's dapper wedding suit of the same.

Tragically, along with the magic, illusion, and beauty of the time, death came to steal the Demented Women as the New Orleans gay community was ravaged by AIDS in the 1980s. Soon, all their drag shows were fundraisers for sick friends.

Fear ran rampant in the early days of the disease, when no one knew the source of the illness that often brought on Kaposi sarcoma lesions, pneumocystis pneumonia, blindness, and eventual death. The medical community suited up as though they were battling bubonic plague in an attempt to protect themselves against the unknown. Dying AIDS patients were shunned even by their families and loved ones.

Father Bob Pawell established the Tau House, a place of Franciscan spirituality, in New Orleans' French Quarter in the mid-1970s. Located at 1029 Governor Nicholls, it became a small faith community that was gay friendly and open to all, especially alienated Catholics. Father Bob was intent on reaching the marginalized fringes of society—many of whom were part of the gay community there. Quickly, Tau House became a place of refuge, especially when black wreaths began to appear on doors across the Quarter and death was clearly all around.

Then, Father Bob received the call that changed everything. A doctor from Charity Hospital phoned to say there was an AIDS patient about to be released from Charity Hospital with nowhere to go. With empty guest rooms at Tau House, Father Bob did what he described later as "living in the yes to life" and welcomed the man into the Franciscan home.

Much to his surprise, the next day the Veterans Administration called to inquire about a hospice they'd heard he had established. That hospice quickly became a reality and in 1985, Lazarus House was founded.

From the earliest days, Sister Marcy Romaine, a Franciscan sister of Our Lady of Perpetual Help, was part of the lifeblood of Lazarus House. With her twinkling eyes and charming smile, Sister Marcy quickly assembled a team of volunteers to assist with errands like doctor's appointments and prescriptions, but most importantly to be present in the lives of the dying men.

So often Sister Marcy would make the phone call to say that a son or a brother was dying, only to be told, "Let us know when he dies" or worse. In the fall of 1985, there were 18 residents at Lazarus House. Eleven men died there that year between Thanksgiving and Christmas. Sister Marcy and her volunteers ensured no one died alone.

This was the New Orleans my beloved friend Joe found upon his return. He'd just served as executive chef of the Mississippi Governor's Mansion under the Mabus administration and was in the midst of a full-blown midlife crisis. After a life spent in professional kitchens, he was searching for a new path.

The after party at a Demented Women's show in the 1980s.
(Courtesy Kathleen Conlon)

Many of Joe's friends had already died from the new plague and many more were sick. In those dark days, Joe was drawn to the Tau House. He began to pray daily with the Franciscan community there, inspired by their mission "to end all forms of prejudice in this lifetime."

When Joe returned to New Orleans, he found our darling Robby Hayward in the end stages of AIDS after having nursed his beloved George through his own death. Joe welcomed Robby into his home and provided hospice care in the sunny dining room of his shotgun house until his death. The Franciscan friars of the Tau House provided spiritual and emotional support during that time.

Father Henry Willenborg, OFM was part of the Tau House community, serving for six years as chaplain of Project Lazarus. He remembers Tau House as "almost acting under the radar of the Archdiocese. We lived the Franciscan way, always considering the loving and compassionate thing to do."

This especially came into play when families refused to claim the bodies of their dead. Sympathetic New Orleans funeral homes provided low-cost cremation and although it was frowned upon by the Catholic Church, the Tau House held services with the cremains. No matter what the religious beliefs of the deceased may have been, a funeral mass was offered on their behalf in the Tau House chapel on Governor Nicholls.

"I'm certain I performed over 100 funerals during my time there," Henry recalled. It's important to note that Father Henry was just one of three priests caring for the community there, so that number easily triples in retrospect.

When Robby died, the Tau House was there to support Joe and Robby's loved ones. Ruby was sent off with full honors from the Demented Women. Glitter was a particular hallmark of their burials, with large quantities of shimmering color freely mixed in with the cremated bits of bones and ash.

At the conclusion of the solemn Catholic burial mass, a small bit of glittery cremains were sprinkled in the garden at the Tau House. The mourners then carried the remains off into the streets of the French Quarter. Stopping at every hangout and watering hole, the survivors hosted their friend for one last dance and one last toast. Then, ceremoniously, a dash of glitter and ash were left behind as the party continued on to the next stop.

That is why, in the New Orleans of the late 1980s and early '90s, whenever you spotted a bit of glitter anywhere—from a bar stool to the flagstone streets—you could never be sure if it had strayed errantly from a costume or mask or if perhaps it was actually just a bit of a Demented Woman.

Poppy Tooker

Acknowledgments

I cannot express my gratitude and admiration for the NO/AIDS Task Force and their amazing work with the New Orleans LGBTQ community. You all were there at the start, and today I am in awe of the way you are growing and expanding both vision and mission through the work of CrescentCare. I am honored to have CrescentCare as my charitable partner on this project.

Special thanks to Noel Twilbeck and Rodney Thouilion for being such wonderful collaborators on all my wacky ideas—like having a little drag brunch in honor of Julian Eltinge. I am also grateful to Michael Weber for having trusted me as celebrity chair with Food for Friends. I miss you, but I hope we're making you proud.

Thanks to the little brother of my heart, Mark Latter, for his incredible generosity in allowing my bevy of drag queens to have Tujague's as their playground while generously donating proceeds to Food for Friends. Poppy's Pop Up Drag Queen Brunch would never have existed without you.

Thank you to both Vinsantos Defonte and José A. Guzman Colón for having magically appeared when it was time to conceive the book's cover. Vince, your work in the New Orleans drag community has touched and brought to life such creative beauty in our next generation of budding queens. And Chef Rich Lee of Antoine's! Thank you for envisioning and executing in rainbow colors the Baked Alaska for the cover.

I owe a deep debt of gratitude to Wayne Phillips of the Louisiana State Museum. His brilliant summary of drag history in New Orleans provided depth and gravitas to this book. Thank you for sharing your brilliant research with us, Wayne!

I owe a special debt of gratitude to all my chef, restaurateur, and foodie friends for their delicious contributions. Our on-site photo shoots, complete with food and drag queens, were graciously accommodated at Antoine's, Brennan's, and Ralph's on the Park. Special thanks to Lisa and Rick Blount, Ralph Brennan, Dickie Brennan and his crew at Tableau and the Palace; Tory McPhail and the teams from Commander's and SoBou; Isaac and Amanda Toups; the amazing Larry Nguyen; and Emery Whalen and Brian Landry of Jack Rose, along with chefs Jarred Zeringue, Tariq Hanna, Michael Gulotta, Thomas Robey, and Susan Spicer.

None of this would have been possible without my drag queen wrangler, Jake Thomas. Not only did Jake wrangle the queens for every Pop Up Drag Brunch, but through his artistic vision he has curated the drag queen print series, all the while raising countless dollars for CrescentCare. Jake's attention to detail and creative genius was an immeasurable help to me as we pushed this project forward.

Kudos to budding chef-ette, my very own Maddy Mouledoux, for her invaluable input with recipe testing. Maddy, your Uncle Joe is proud of you. By the way, the stand mixer you used in recipe testing originally belonged to my friend and Demented Woman, Robby (Ruby) Hayward.

So many dear friends helped in so many ways. Kit Wohl was always there with great advice. Anne Garner never fails with her fearless suggestions when faced with pages of my prose. Julie Mabus was dogged in her pursuit of the archival photo of Joe, taken when he was chef and she was first lady of Mississippi. Kathleen Conlon, one of the few surviving Demented Women, appeared magically to share her memories of those long-ago days.

Thanks to Sally Asher for drag show photobombing. Your eye made such a difference. Big thanks to Charlotte Tobin for her fresh, new design ideas and to my publisher, Scott Campbell, and his talented team for sharing my vision of what this book should be.

Sam Hanna proved to be so much more than a photographer on this project. Sam shares his art and vision on every page. With the help of New Orleans' finest chefs and restaurateurs, Sam and I did guerilla tactics photo shoots, accomplishing the book's food photography in its entirety in just three days! Sam, I couldn't have done it without you—truly!

But most of all, thanks for all the help that appeared, almost miraculously throughout this entire fast-paced project. Those thanks, I believe, are owed directly to divine intervention from my beloved Joe and all the Demented Women. That must be some drag show they're putting on in heaven!

Index

Award-winning author, media personality, educator, and culinary historian Poppy Tooker was born and bred in the birthplace of brunch—New Orleans. Poppy is passionate about food and the people who bring it to the table. Her books include the award-winning titles *Crescent City Farmers Market Cookbook; Louisiana Eats! The People, the Food and Their Stories; Madame Begue's Recipes of Old New Orleans Creole Cookery; Tujague's Cookbook;* and *Pascal's Manale Cookbook.* She hosts the weekly syndicated radio program *Louisiana Eats!* and on lucky weekends, you can find Poppy hosting charity drag queen brunch fun throughout her beloved city. Learn more about Poppy at poppytooker.com.

(Courtesy Sam Hanna)

Sam Hanna is a New Orleans-based culinary photographer with an extensive list of local and national clients ranging from boutique eateries and bakeries to national branded food products. With nearly 20 years in the publishing industry, Sam made the move to New Orleans from Detroit in 2008 to specialize in culinary photography and has photographed cookbooks and cover photos for national and local publications. See more of Hanna's work at hannafoto.com.

(Courtesy Sandra O'Claire)

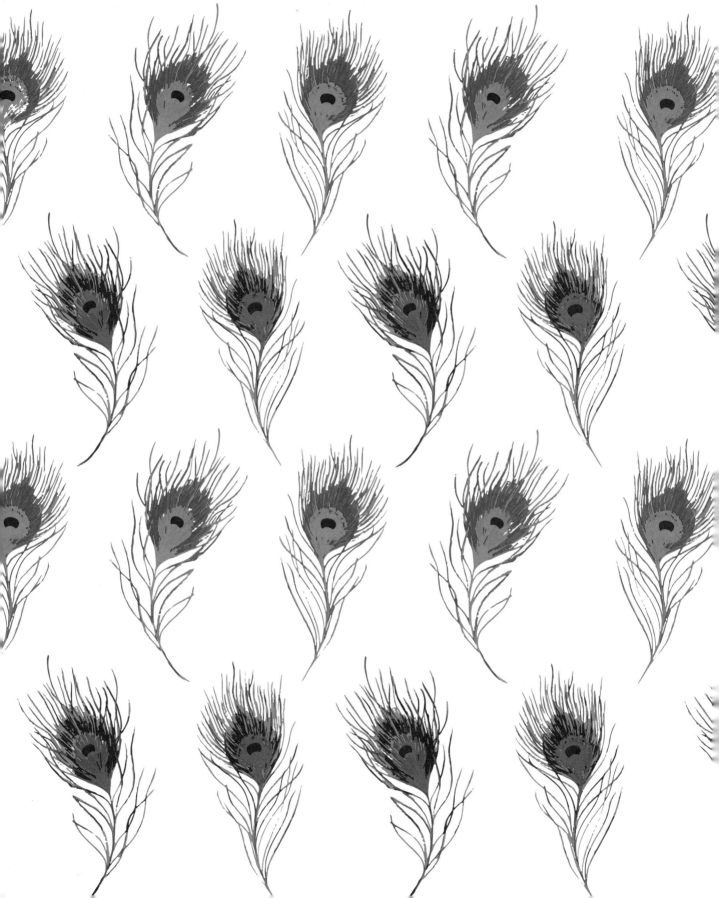